The Practical Handbook of
REMODELING
and
HOME IMPROVEMENTS
By John Capotosto

Fawcett Publications, Inc.
1515 Broadway
New York, New York 10036

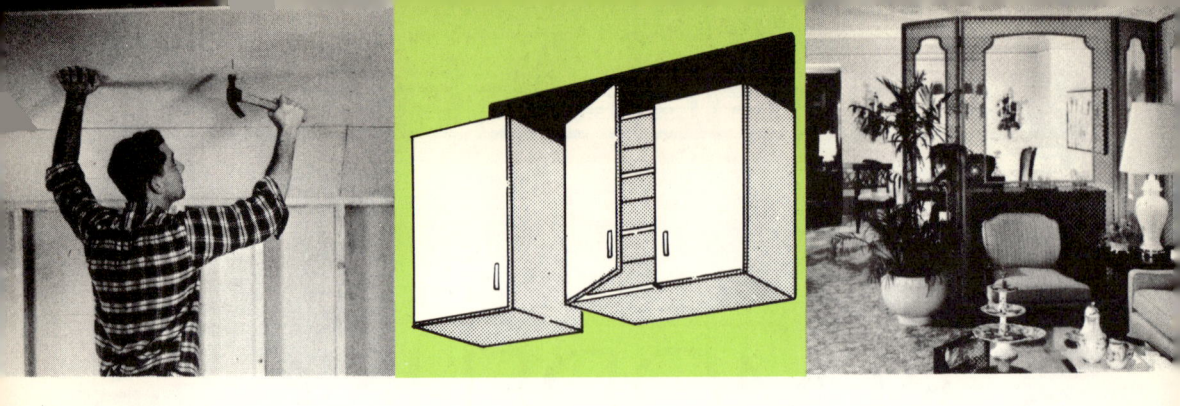

FRANK BOWERS: *Editor-in-Chief*

WILLIAM MIUCCIO: *Art Editor*

MICHAEL GAYNOR: *Asst. Art Editor* • HAROLD E. PRICE: *Art Coordinator, Special Projects*

JOSEPH C. PENELL: *Marketing Director*

LARRY H. WERLINE: *Editor*

Editorial Staff: DAN BLUE, ELLENE SAUNDERS, JOE CORONA, JAMES WYCKOFF, MARSHA STEIN, COLLEEN KATZ, MARION LYONS

Art Staff: ALEX SANTIAGO, JOHN SELVAGGIO, JOHN CERVASIO, JACK LA CERRA, AL JETTER, CHARLIE TAUBLIEB, EDWARD WERTH

LEDA BARRY: *Production Editor*

How-To Art by Henry Clark
Cover Color by John Capotosto
All photos not credited are by the author

No part of this book may be reproduced in any form without permission in writing from the publisher, except by a reviewer who wishes to quote brief passages in connection with a review written for inclusion in a magazine, newspaper or broadcast.

Printed in U.S.A. by
FAWCETT PRINTING CORPORATION
Rockville, Maryland

Copyright © MCMLXXIII by Fawcett Publications, Inc.
All Rights Reserved

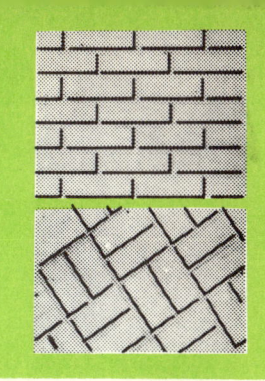

CONTENTS

Remodeling: Where to Begin?	4
Walls Are For Covering	6
Wallpapers and Fabrics	24
Fabrics For Fashionable Wall Coverings	28
Skin For a Dull Door	30
Stretch That Storage Space	32
Paints and Painting	38
Installing Wallboard	41
Factory-Built, Wall-Hung Fireplace	44
Combination Room Divider-Fireplace	45
Focus On Floors	48
Window Cover-Ups	56
A Rustic Den	62
Kitchen Capers	65
Close-up On Ceilings	69
Attics and Basements	73
Beauty In Boxes	78
Wall Accessories	87
Early American Clock	94
Mounting A Picture	96
Accent Walls	98
Tips On Dividers	100
Why Wood Windows	106
New For the Bathroom	109
Create With Spindles	113
Decorating with Tape	116
Build a Coffee Table	118
Instant Magic	121
List of Sources For Materials	124
Index	125

Ethan Allen

In a quandry? Will you paper that wall and paint this one? Or should you panel that wall and knock this one down? Tile floor or brick? Look, let's start over and really plan this thing...

REMODELING: WHERE TO BEGIN?

Plan the improvement carefully, estimate costs and compare products

Home remodeling and improving covers a lot of territory. More than two billion dollars are spent by homeowners every year on do-it-yourself home improvement projects. Quite an impressive figure. Most of this money is spent wisely, especially when the homeowner has taken the time to carefully plan the improvement, estimate the costs and compare the various products offered.

The first question you should ask yourself is, are you qualified to tackle the job yourself? Some remodeling and improvement projects are best left to the professional. Unless you have the experience, major electrical and plumbing jobs should be left to the experts. Even some room remodeling may require the help of a professional. For example, walls are easier to put up than to remove. If a wall is load-bearing, you may pull half the house down with the wall. Doing the work yourself may not always be the cheapest way.

The projects in this book have been

While not essential, stationery power tools come in mighty handy when doing home improvement projects. While the initial cost may be high, the time and labor saved are well worth it. Spending a little more pays.

Georgia-Pacific

A well-equipped workshop will help you turn out quality workmanship. This shop, while small, will handle most remodeling jobs with ease. While stationary tools are not necessary, some portables are a must.

One problem facing the remodeler is making the decision of what product to use. There are hundreds to choose from and this can be just as bad as having too few.

chosen with the thought that they can be easily tackled by the average homeowner who wishes to remodel his home without the expense of professional labor. It should also assist those who can afford professional workmanship, to better judge the quality of products offered and to suggest ways to make your home a more comfortable and pleasant place in which to live. Follow the ideas in this book or they may spark creative adaptations or new ideas of your own.

Sketches of your planned remodeling project are important. Get as much information on the subject as you can from manufacturers' brochures, home improvement books and magazines. Discuss your plans with your building materials dealer; he knows the mistakes that most amateurs make and can offer you some good technical advice.

When selecting products for your remodelling, choose wisely. The more expensive item may prove the most economical in the long run. Generally, the costlier materials will last longer and give you years of trouble-free service. This is not always the case however, so be inquisitive. Ask questions and learn as much as you can about a product. Find out how much it costs, how it can be applied, is it durable, what colors are available, etc. Most important of all, do you like it and do you really want to live with it?

Marlite

Modern look is not difficult to achieve with new materials. Textured paneling on family room wall has a plastic-coated surface and is easily wiped clean with a damp cloth.

WALLS ARE FOR COVERING

If your walls bore you, read on. . . .

More often than not, walls are boring to look at. They serve as a backdrop for furniture when they should actually be adding visual interest, providing dramatic accent or emphasizing the room decor.

One way to alter this situation is to panel them with prefinished paneling, such as hardboard, wood paneling, imitation stone, tiles, wallpapers, and fabrics.

For touches of glamor, filigree hardboards offer an excellent choice. Use them in bathrooms, foyers, and bedrooms. Use them for accent paneling, room dividers, and folding screens.

Textured panels may be used in recreation areas, hobby rooms and hallways. Try the embossed panels in dining areas and the marbelized for the bathrooms. Many styles and colors are available. We show some ideas on these pages. Adapt these or create your own.

INSTALLING PANELS

Panels can be installed on existing walls if they are sound and flat, otherwise furring strips will be required. Ordinary tools are all you need although the use of power tools will make the job go faster. To determine the number of panels required, simply add the lengths of the walls and divide by four if your panels are 48" wide. Deduct half a panel for doors and ¼ panel for windows.

If wood-grained panels are used, they should be arranged for the best grain effect. Line the panels up around the room and arrange them for grain and color sequence. Number the back of the panels with a crayon in the sequence in which you will use them. Condition the panels by leaving them standing in the room for 48 hours prior to installation. This will acclimate them to the room's temperature and humidity.

Panel installation differs slightly depending on the type used. Plywood panels are butted and hardboard is installed with a slight gap at the joints.

The installation of the paneling is not too difficult. Except for areas around doors and windows, the installation is fairly fast. If the walls being covered are fairly flat, the panels can be mounted directly using adhesives. Walls in bad condition will require furring strips. These should run at right angles to the direction of the panel application. Mount them horizontally, 16" on centers. Furring can be either 1 x 2 lumber or ⅜ x 1⅞ plywood. If necessary, furring should be shimmed to true up the surface. In extreme cases, it may be necessary to use 2 x 3 studs.

BASEMENT WALLS

Masonry walls in basement may pose a problem because of dampness. If conditions warrant, cure the dampness problem with suitable compounds. These are available at hardware and building supply dealers. In addition, you will need a vinyl vapor barrier and insulation between the masonry surface and your wall. Follow the manufacturer's recommendations for these products.

A barren entry hall was made elegant by covering the walls with Georgia-Pacific Chateau Pecan panels. Contrasting dark brown molding was used for trim around doors and edges.

First step in paneling a room is to make it ready. Carefully remove moldings, switch and outlet plates. If molding is in good shape, you can repaint it to match panels.

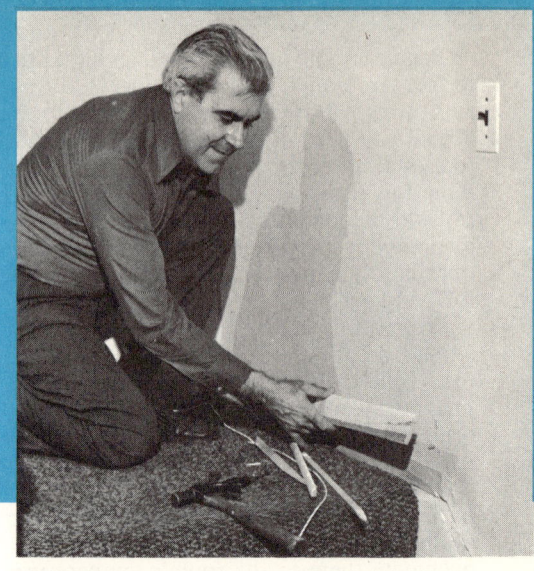

Remove base with care. Here phone line was hidden behind the molding. If possible, tuck wires behind wallboard so they won't be accidentally struck by nails or screws.

Cardboard templates permit you to cut the panels accurately for a perfect fit. Use small pieces of board, taping them into place wherever wall is irregular. Make it exact.

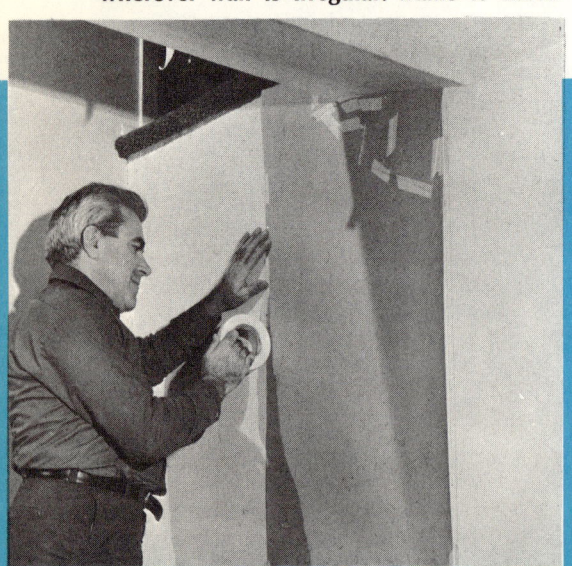

Place panels in room 48 hours before installation to acclimate them to room temperature and humidity. Place in order for best grain patterning; number on back.

8

Butt the first panel to adjacent wall of starting corner. Chances are corner is not plumb. Mark a plumb line at panel's outside edge. Start first panel parallel to this plumb line.

When working to an outside corner, cut the panel so it falls just short of the corner. Outside corner molding will conceal the joint. If you are real handy, you can miter corners.

Remove all moldings around doors, windows, and floor. Remove carefully so they may be reused. If pipes or other obstructions are present, which are not to be relocated, box them in with suitable lumber.

POINTERS ON PROCEDURES

Always start the paneling at a corner. You will find that most corners are not plumb or true. Position the panel into the corner using a level to assure that it is plumb vertically. Tack the panel temporarily and scribe the corner with a compass. Trim the scribed line then install the panel. Allow a slight space at top and bottom for expansion (Moldings will cover these).

When adhesives are used it's a good idea to drive a few nails at the top and bottom of the panel where they will be hidden by the moldings.

Cutting panels: Here are some tips for cutting panels. Mark the panels with a grease pencil or anything that will wipe clean. Hand or power saws may be used to cut panels. Use a crosscut handsaw to prevent splintering. *Do the cutting only on the down stroke.* Power saws should be fitted with a hollow ground blade. On table saws, keep the panel face up while cutting. On portable or bayonet type saws, panel face should be down. *A strip of masking tape on the cutting line will keep splintering to a minimum.*

Prefinished moldings to match your paneling are available. These include inside corner, outside corner, base, cove and the necessary door and window trim. Metal moldings are also available for use with hardboard paneling. In addition to the above, metal moldings also include edge, divider and end caps.

UNTRUE OLD WALLS

The following instructions pertain to old walls which are not "true."

Furring strips should be applied so that they run at right angles to the direction of panel application. Furring strips of 3/8" x 1 7/8" plywood strips or 1" x 2" lumber should be used. If either plaster, masonry or other type of wall is uneven such that it cannot be trued up by using furring

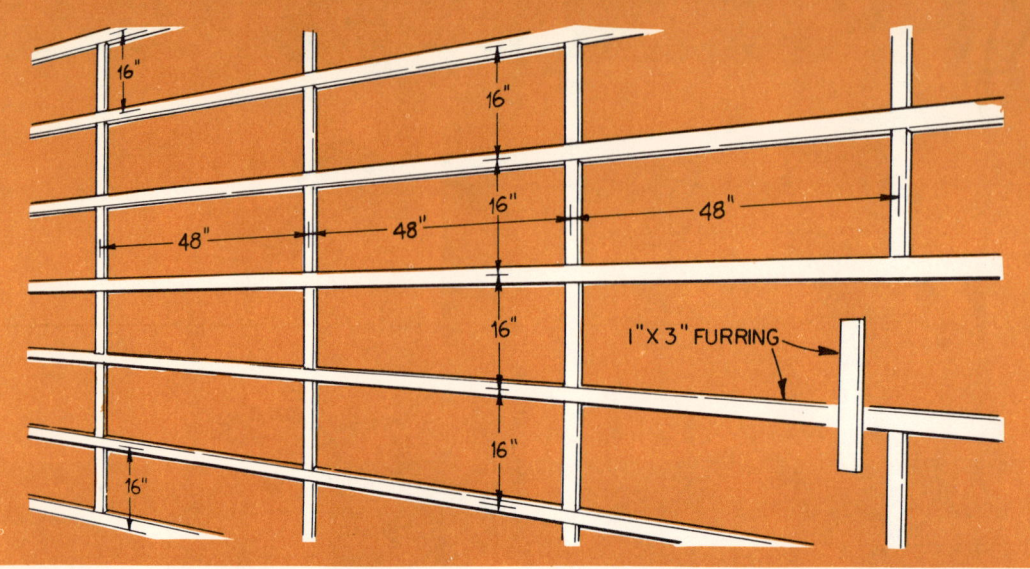

Furring a wall is an important part of a paneling installation. Vertical strips must be spaced 48" on center to support panel edges. Horizontal strips are usually 16" apart.

strips and shimming them out where wall bellows; 2" x 3" studs may be necessary.

You can use studs flat against the wall in order to conserve space. Use studs for top and bottom plates and space vertical studs 16" on center. Apply paneling direct to studs or over gypsum or plywood backerboard. Solid backing is required along all four panel edges of each panel.

Add strips wherever needed to insure this support. It is a good idea to place bottom furring strip ½" from floor. Leave a ¼" space between the horizontal strips and the vertical strips to allow for some ventilation.

MASONRY WALLS

Use masonry nails to apply horizontal furring strips every 16" beginning ¼" above floor level. Insert vertical strips to support panel edges. Shim as needed to obtain flush surface (wood shingles make ideal shims.) Allow clearance of at least ½" above top furring strip and below bottom furring strip. This space should be provided below horizontal strips between each run of vertical strips.

Attach furring to masonry by drilling holes and inserting wood plugs or expansion shield, then nailing or screwing furring into the plugs or shields. Hardened cut nails, nail or bolt anchors or adhesive anchors can also be used, so can one of the new powder-actuated fastening systems now available.

PLASTER WALLS

Nail strips to studs horizontally starting at the floor line and continuing up wall every 16". Nail vertical strips, also every 4' to support panel edges. Level uneven areas by placing shims (pieces of shingle make excellent shims) behind the furring strips to level.

FURRING

If walls to be paneled are in poor condition, you will have to "fur" out the wall. Furring strips are available in 1" x 2" or 1" x 3" strips. They are inexpensive and they come in various lengths. Install the furring 16" on center horizontally and 48" vertically. The vertical strips will support the panel edges so place them accurately.

Start the first vertical strip so that its center is exactly 48" from the corner of the adjacent wall. When applying furring to masonry walls, you can use either masonry nails or adhesive. If nails are used, be sure to wear protective goggles to protect your eyes. Masonry nails are very

American Hardboard Assoc.

On bad walls, space furring 16" on center horizontally and 48" on center vertically. Use shims to level off face of strips. Hardboard panels can be applied with adhesive.

Before installing first hardboard panel be sure it is plumb by checking with level. Use of adhesive eliminates nails. If nails are used, select annular-thread or ring-grooved ones.

brittle and if they break while being installed, they can cause considerable damage.

For uneven walls, insert shims to even out the furring. Shingles are ideal for this purpose because of their wedge shape. If paneling is to be installed on exterior masonry walls, the wall must be waterproofed with a waterproofing paint and then a vapor barrier installed. Thin plastic film is available for this purpose.

Most lumber dealers and building supply homes carry the film in several thicknesses. The heavier material costs more, but it is well worth the added cost for it's far more durable than lighter-gauge material. The vapor barrier is installed on the wall before the furring is applied.

THE SECRETS OF WORKING WITH MOLDING

The secret of a good-looking molding job is in making accurate measurements. Ceiling and base moldings will not necessarily be the same length. If the walls are off plumb, these measurements will vary. Measure each piece individually and use a sharp saw blade on your power saw or, if you use a miter box, use a back-

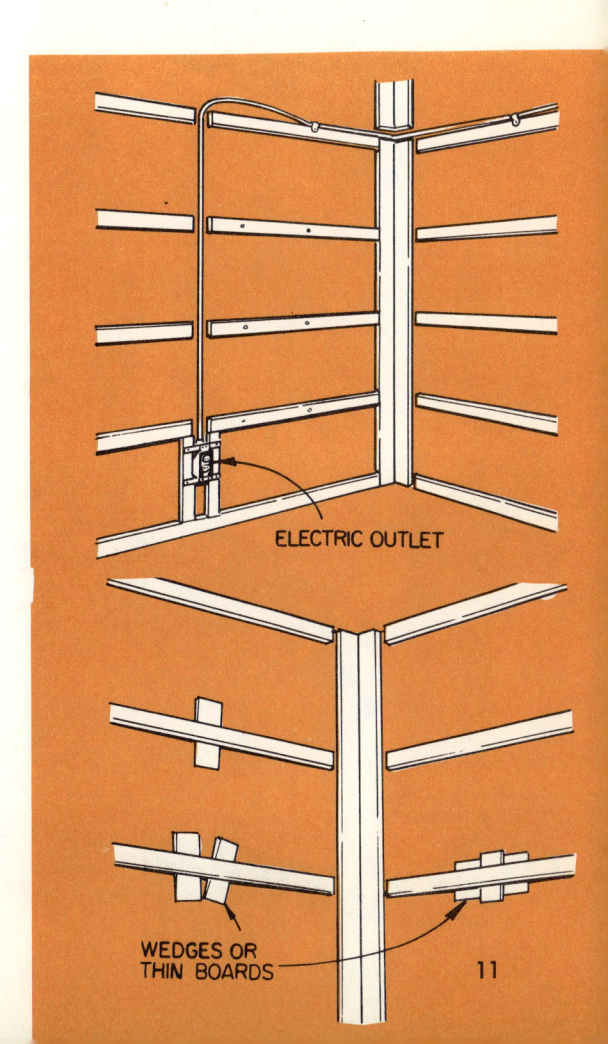

ELECTRIC OUTLET

WEDGES OR THIN BOARDS

11

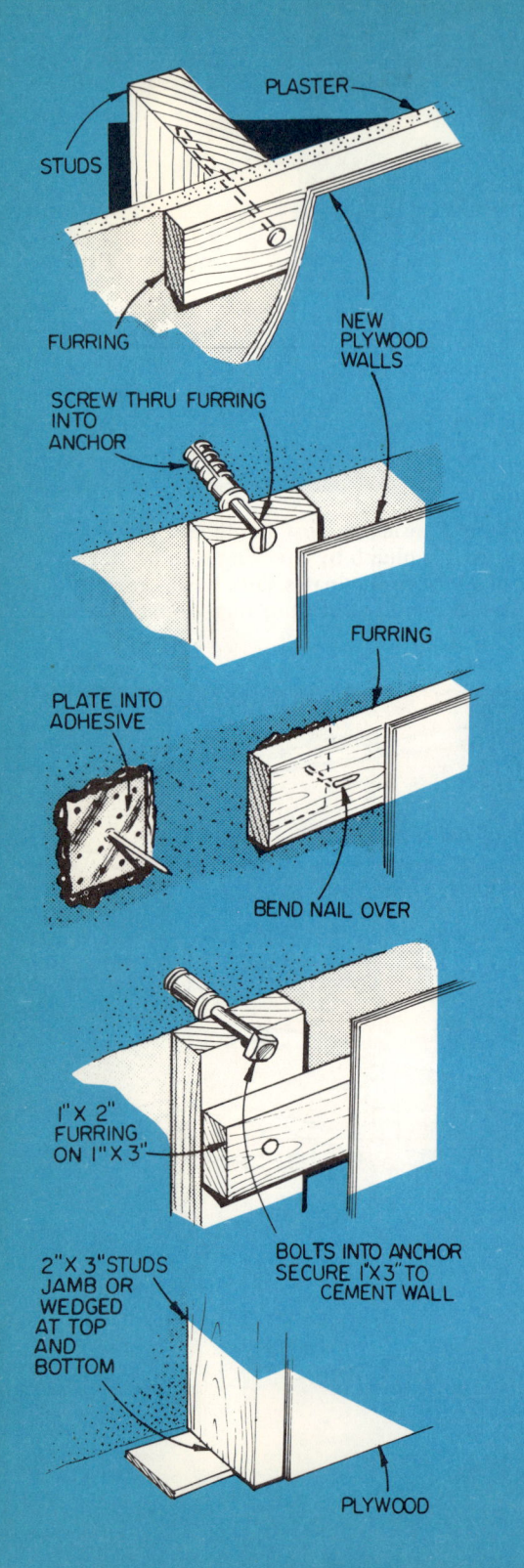

saw which is especially designed for cutting moldings.

Most moldings are cut in either a vertical or horizontal position, whichever is convenient. There is an exception, however, and this is when mitering crown or cove moldings. These must be held in the same position when cutting as they will have when mounted.

The best way to position the molding on the saw or in the miter box is to nail a strip of wood to the saw table, or inside the miter box. The strip of wood acts as a stop thus supporting the molding in the proper position while cutting.

While cove moldings are specified for use at the joint between wall and ceiling, casing or stop moldings may also be used. These lay flat and are easy to apply.

If a ceiling height is greater than the standard panel, a cap molding may be used to finish off the top of the panels. Cap molding may also be used around doors and windows when remodeling. The cap is rabbeted to allow for the thickness of the panels. Ordinary casing may also be used but it will have to be rabbeted as indicated on the drawing.

The same casing molding used around doors and windows may be used as a base molding. Generally the two are identical in shape with the base being wider of the two.

When necessary to splice a molding, to increase its length along the same wall, it is advisable to make 45° cuts on both pieces.

When nailing moldings use 3-penny finish nails and sink heads then fill with a putty stick in matching color. Colored nails may also be used thus eliminating the sinking and filling operation.

MOLDINGS

Factory-finished moldings simplify an otherwise tedious job. You no longer need to sand, fill, stain and finish them for all of this is taken care of by the manufacturer. Moldings can be installed to match the paneling on a wall, or in a pleasing contrasting color or tone.

While moldings are designed for specific applications, there are no fast hard rules. Casing is generally used to trim doors and windows, but it may also be used in place of base and ceiling moldings.

The factory applied finish is very tough and will resist kicks and bumps, and wipe clean wth a damp cloth. Scratches and mars from hard use are easily eliminated by using a matching putty stick.

When measuring a room for paneling, be sure to measure around doors and windows for molding footage. Molding should be purchased when buying the paneling so that it can be compared with the panel for selection of the best harmonizing or contrasting tone.

Here are the most common moldings and their uses: Cove or ceiling molding is used where paneling meets the ceiling. It gives the room a finished appearance and conceals irregular ceiling lines. Cap molding is used to cover exposed panel edges, such as the top of wainscot-height panels. Outside corner guard finishes the outside corners by covering the joints and seams. It lends a finished appearance to a paneled room.

Casing is used to trim doors and windows. It is similar in appearance to base molding but somewhat narrower. Base and shoe moldings are applied around the perimeter of a room at the intersection of the walls and floor. The shoe is somewhat

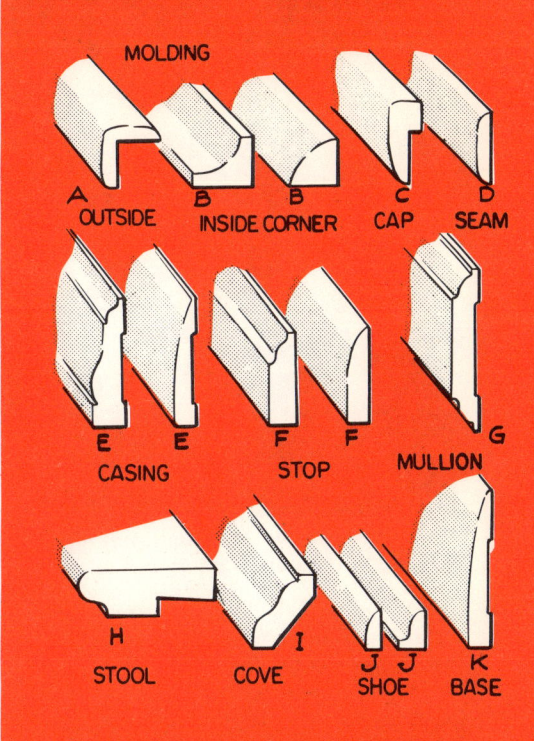

The moldings above are standard and are available at most lumber yards and home improvement centers. The placement of the various shapes is shown below in art.

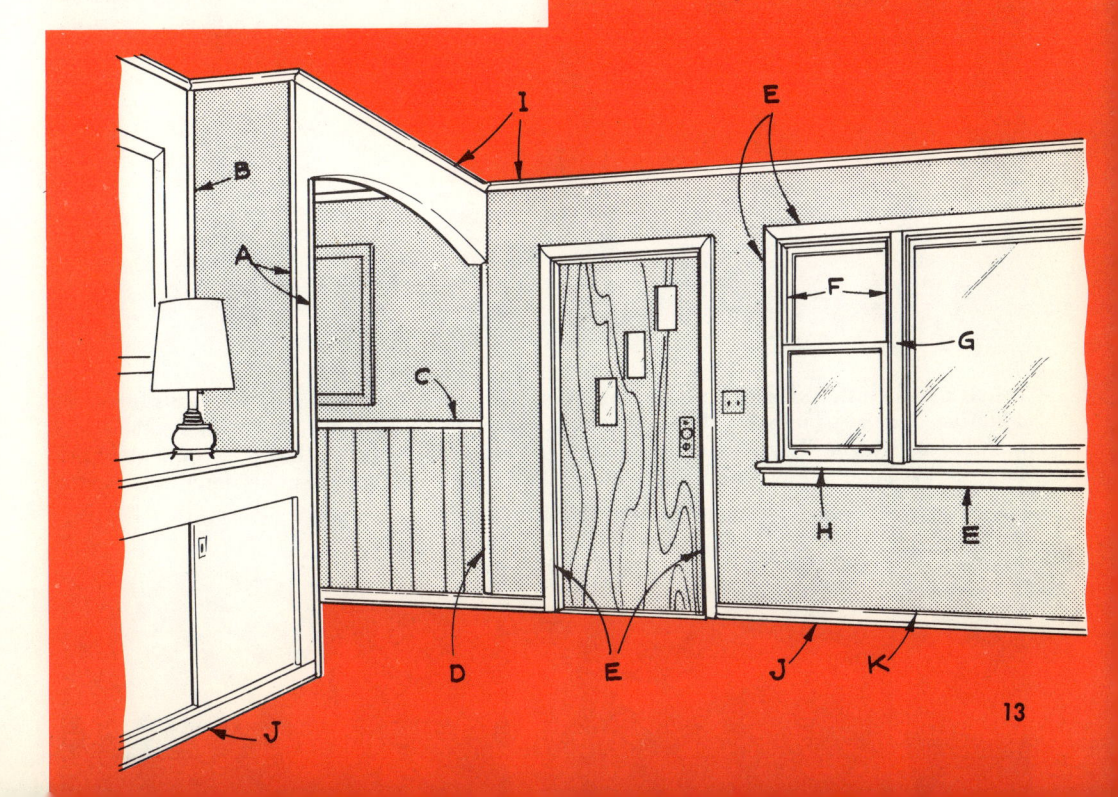

13

Ideal boys room boasts tough prefinished washable travertine hardboard paneling. Built-in shelves and desk are framed and edged with contrasting dark molding—for a lovely effect.

Before installing hardboard paneling, they should be preconditioned by standing them around the room for 24 hours before they are used. Stand so air can circulate around.

Panel adhesives are applied with a caulking gun. Apply adhesive in a broken line on each of the intermediate members. Apply continuous strip of adhesive to perimeter.

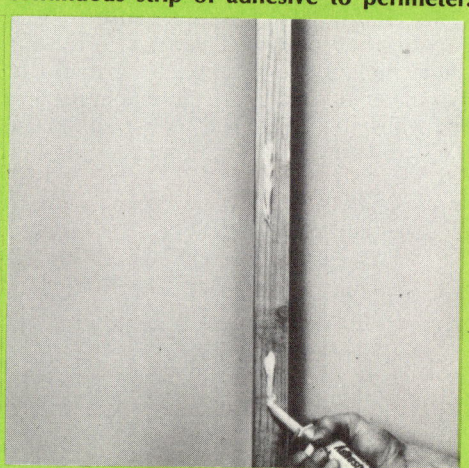

Panels can be installed with nails instead of adhesive. Special paneling nails are recommended as they will not work loose and they are available in many matching colors.

To prevent the possibility of walls buckling, panels must be installed with a small space between them. A thin coin or matchbook is an excellent way to determine space.

The materials available to the do-it-yourselfer are almost limitless. Local lumber yards and building material centers can offer many ideas. Brochures are also helpful too.

An experienced lumber dealer can effectively advise you on the newest materials available, and how best to use them. Discussing your plans save time and money.

flexible and can be installed to conform to uneven floors.

Seam or batten moldings are used to cover vertical and horizontal joints where two panels butt.

Stop molding is used to finish door and window openings. They keep windows in

For something different, try installing panels with the grooves running horizontally or combine both as was done here. Tiles around fire place is also a very novel idea.

their tracks and prevent doors from swinging through the door frames.

PREFINISHED MOLDINGS

Prefinished wood moldings "finish" paneling installations. They trim door and window openings to complement paneled walls; cover seams and joints at ceilings, floors, corners and other areas and protect paneling from kicks and bumps. They harmonize with paneling, and have a tough surface finish that resists dirt absorption and is easily cleaned with a damp rag or sponge.

Their factory applied finish eliminates the need for finishing on the job. Scratches and mars from hard use are quickly repaired with a colored putty stick. Easily worked and installed with common woodworking tools, wood moldings are the final step in a paneling installation.

They are available in lengths engineered to reduce installation waste even for novice do-it-yourselfers.

When measuring a room for paneling, additional measurements around doors, windows and other areas give molding footage requirements. To insure enough molding for each 45-degree cut measure the width of the molding, round off to the next higher foot and add to the total required footage.

The best time to buy prefinished moldings is when the paneling is purchased, since the material requirements for both products will already be known. Also, the molding may be compared with paneling for quick selection of the best harmonizing or contrasting color tones.

CORNERS

The following diagrams show the easy way to place moldings in corners, at the ceiling and floor, around windows and doors or for wainscoting. If your walls are over 8' high you can use a molding at the joint where the additional panel is stacked over your 8' panel.

Marlite

Tongue and groove panels 16" wide and 8' tall go up fast and easy. Panels are mounted with adhesive and clips. Clips assure proper spacing in between to allow for expansion.

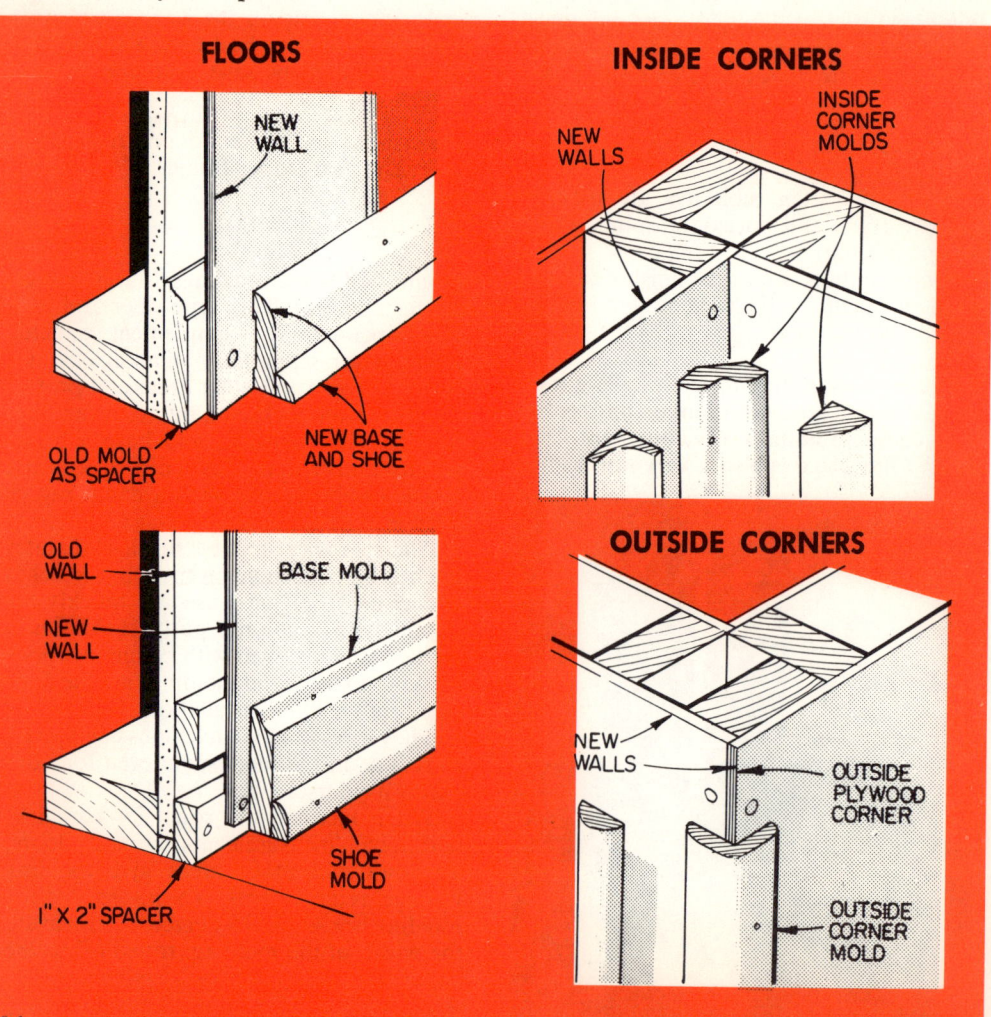

FLOORS

NEW WALL
OLD MOLD AS SPACER
NEW BASE AND SHOE

OLD WALL
NEW WALL
BASE MOLD
SHOE MOLD
1" X 2" SPACER

INSIDE CORNERS

NEW WALLS
INSIDE CORNER MOLDS

OUTSIDE CORNERS

NEW WALLS
OUTSIDE PLYWOOD CORNER
OUTSIDE CORNER MOLD

DOORS AND WINDOWS

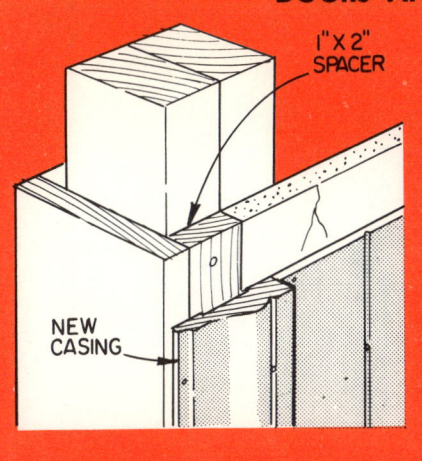

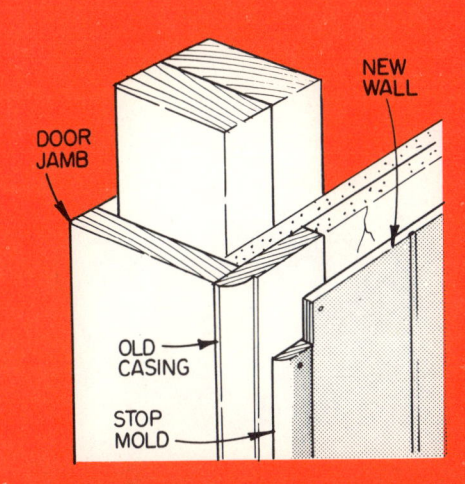

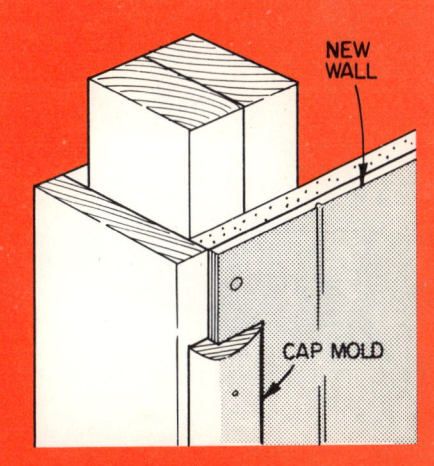

CEILINGS

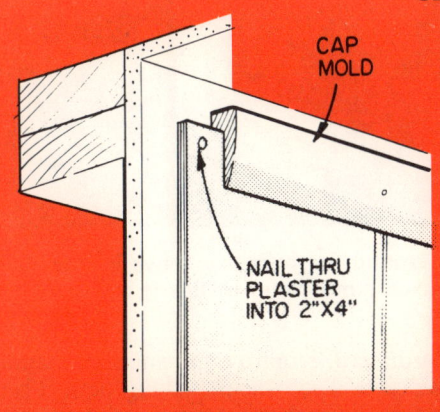

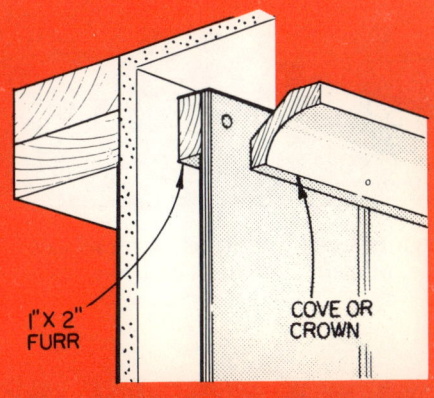

Drawings above show solutions to typical problems. If old casing is removed, you can either use a cap molding or cut a rabbet in the new casing to match the new wall.

17

American Plywood Association

Rough textured wall paneling forms suitable background for primitive artwork over fireplace. Modern furniture completes the casual relaxed atmosphere of this spacious room.

POINTERS ON CARE

Walls covered with prefinished paneling, whether it be wood or decorative hardboard, require a minimum of maintenance to keep them looking new. These special finishes resist stain and mars.

If the panels must be cleaned, the use

Plastic-finished, carved-leaf panels used around fireplace create a striking accent wall. Rectangular panels were trimmed to proper size and then cemented to the solid backing.

of a damp cloth is all that is usually needed. For stubborn pencil and crayon marks, the use of a mild detergent may be required. When soil is removed, rinse and allow to dry thoroughly then apply a clear wax.

Never use a cleanser with a coarse abrasive, it may damage the surface of the panel. Cleansers or waxes which leave a deposit in the pores of the wood must not be used. If the paneling is textured, a heavy cloth should be used so the fibers won't catch in the wood grain.

COVERING UP BLEMISHES

Should a scratch or marring occur on a prefinished panel, it may be necessary to refinish the damaged area. If the damage is severe, it would be best to call in an expert to do the refinishing. Slight scratches can usually be handled with a putty stick. These are available in matching colors and they are simply rubbed over the scratch. The scratch will fill with the special putty and in most cases the repair is invisible.

If only the finish was damaged, use a clear wax, applying it with a damp cloth and rubbing with the grain.

Wood, like most other materials, is sensitive to light to some degree. Fortunately panels mellow with age under the influence of light. However, if pictures are hung flat on the wall, the area behind the picture will not mellow with the rest of the wall, resulting in a lighter area behind the picture.

To minimize this effect, pictures should be hung about ½" away from the wall. This can easily be done by placing nails into the rear of the frame. This will permit light to seep behind the picture eliminating the sharp contrasts.

A SELECTION OF BRICK PATTERNS—

Brick may be laid in a variety of patterns. Here are some of the more commonly used. There are no fast and hard rules that must be followed. Why not try vertical application?

Decorating her own room will delight any teenager. These 1' x 2' brick panels are quickly and easily applied. The bulletin board is of self-sticking natural cork tiles.

Decro-wall Corp.

Artificial stones in various styles are also available. These are applied in the same manner as the bricks. Stones and bricks can be cut with a hacksaw, nippers or table saw. Imitation brick or stone walls are easier to install and maintain, more economical, and much lighter in weight than the genuine materials. They are ideal for fireplace outer walls, and rooms where a rustic or Early American style is desired.

"Instant bricklaying for everyone." That's how the ads read and it's true! Anyone can lay brick using the new high-density polyester bricks. They are only ¼" thick, but they look and feel like the real thing.

That's not all. The adhesive used to apply the bricks looks just like mortar and it has the same texture when dry. Three easy steps are involved. Spread a thin coat

Looks like brick, feels like real brick, but isn't. It's a decorative brick facing, synthetically made of polyester. Each is ¼" thick, weighs only 4 ounces—for easy use.

Brick may be applied to any interior surface that is structurally sound, dry and clean. Putty knife is used to spread a thin coat of mortar over the entire surface to be "bricked."

Just before installing the brick, use a putty knife to butter the back cavity of each brick with adhesive mortar. Shallow cavity takes little mortar but must be completely filled.

Buttered bricks are pressed into position. Wiggle slightly from side to side to make certain they are firmly embedded. Mortar should be allowed to ooze from all 4 sides.

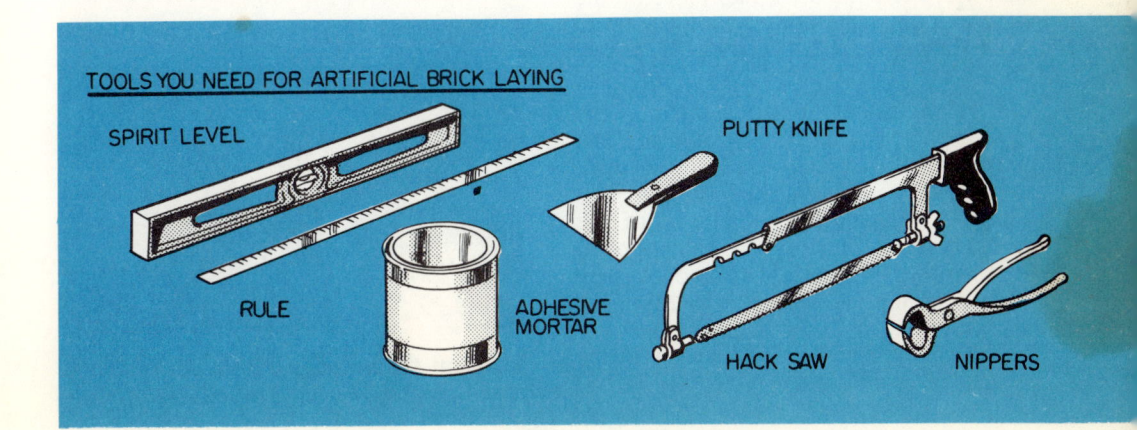

TOOLS YOU NEED FOR ARTIFICIAL BRICK LAYING

SPIRIT LEVEL
RULE
ADHESIVE MORTAR
PUTTY KNIFE
HACK SAW
NIPPERS

21

New decorative brick material comes in a can. Bricks are spread on wall with a trowel. The mortar lines and brick shapes are formed with a special tape (later removed).

Dacor Manufacturing Co., Inc.

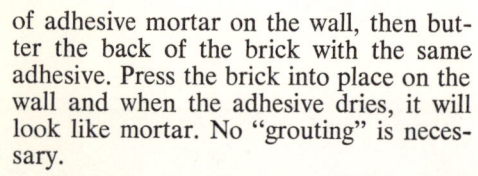

After stirring base coat, use a putty knife or trowel to spread it out in a thin, even coat.

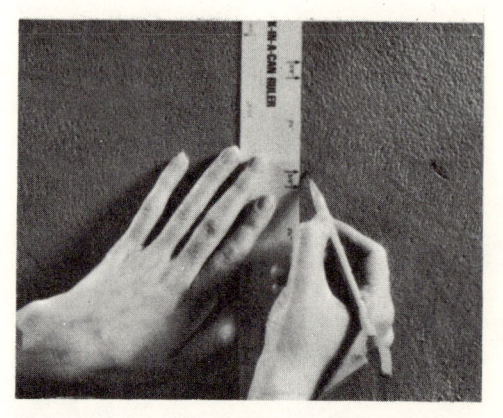

Using special ruler furnished, place it against wall and mark off mortar lines as indicated.

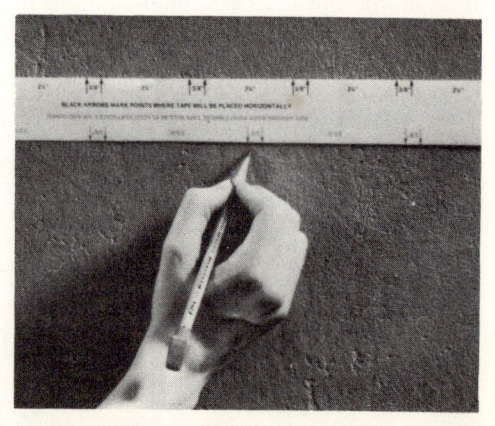

Mark off the horizontal lines with ruler. If area is wider than ruler, move ruler, repeat.

of adhesive mortar on the wall, then butter the back of the brick with the same adhesive. Press the brick into place on the wall and when the adhesive dries, it will look like mortar. No "grouting" is necessary.

Another instant brick available to the remodeler is called Brick-In-A-Can. The material is actually troweled onto a wall. A special base coat is first applied, followed by taping which will produce the mortar joint. A finish coat is then applied with a trowel. When the finish coat begins to dry, the tape is peeled away revealing authentic brick and mortar lines.

The material is available in three colors, red, beige, and white.

Run stick-on tape between series of horizontal markings, at ends overlap about 2".

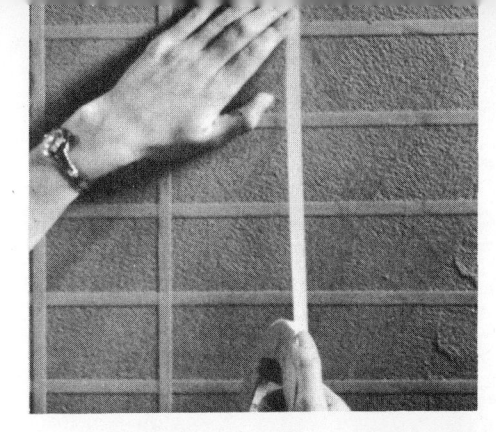

Tape is now applied vertically. Again leave a 2" overhang at the ends for handling ease.

With razor blade, cut through vertical tape where it crosses over each horizontal tape.

Remove every other strip of vertical tape to form the brick shapes as shown in photo.

Spread the finish coat on entire wall with trowel. Spread out, let dry for three hours.

Remove tape by pulling on overlap left at ends of each row, to expose mortar joints.

Richard Thibaut, Inc.
Colorful murals are an excellent way to grace an otherwise dull wall. They add interest and depth, and set the mood or style of a room just as any fine painting accents and enhances.

WALLPAPERS AND FABRICS

Brighten your walls with the new decorator papers and fabrics

Wallcoverings—in vinyl, fabric and paper—are excellent for transforming a dull room into an exciting showplace. Be budget-wise and do the work yourself. You'll find it's easy especially with the new pretrimmed, prepasted materials. The colors, patterns and textures are unlimited. Take your pick of foils, velvets, burlaps, prints, etc.

Mix-or-match wallcoverings—make one wall a printed fabric, contrasting with a wood-paneled room. Or make one wall a brilliant burlap as a background for your photos or pictures. The sky's the limit when you plan your own room decor.

MATERIALS YOU'LL NEED

Papers and vinyls are hung in much the same way. Here's what you'll need: a table or other flat surface to work on (a door on sawhorses will be fine); a stepladder; plumb line; yardstick; straight edge; scissors; razor and screwdriver.

You'll also need: paste brush; smoothing brush; seam roller; paste; sizing and a bucket.

24

TIPS ON PAPERING

• Walls should be clean and free of cracks and holes. Fill crevices with spackle. Remove old wallcoverings unless they are on good and tight. To insure proper adhesion, walls should be sized.

• For covering uneven or imperfect walls, textured or heavily patterned papers are recommended. Foils and the new wet-look vinyls must be hung on perfectly flat, smooth walls.

• As mentioned in the section on paneling, most walls are not straight so the use of a plumb bob in hanging the first strip is most important. If the first strip is hung properly, the rest will follow. Always cut strips about 4″ longer than the height of the wall to allow for trimming. It is a good idea to mark the top of the sheet on the back of the strips. If a pattern is non-matching, every other strip should be reversed to allow for variations in shading.

• When handling papers and foils, *be careful not to crease the material.*

• When hanging the strips, work the smoothing brush from the center out. *Be sure the edges are well pasted.*

• *Use caution* when working *around switches and outlets.* The procedure is to cut an "X" in the paper over the object. *Turn off the power* when making the cut-out as your knife or razor could make contact with the electrical connections inside the box. This of course could cause an electrical shock.

• Foils are metallic and should be installed carefully at the switches and outlets. Cut away excess material. *Do not leave loose ends under the cover plate.*

Fabrics with interesting texture and colors make great wall coverings. With a spark of imagination and a few yards of fabric you can really "turn-on" a room.

In the past, fabrics were glued to walls, but this was always a mess and results weren't always good. Wrinkles were a big problem as were air pockets. Another bad feature was that if the fabric were to be taken down, the entire surface of the wall was left coated with glue. For more on fabrics see our next chapter.

Sometimes you can break the rules effectively as was done here. Paper was purposely hung off plumb. Use contrasting colors alternately. Don't overdo, 2 walls are plenty.

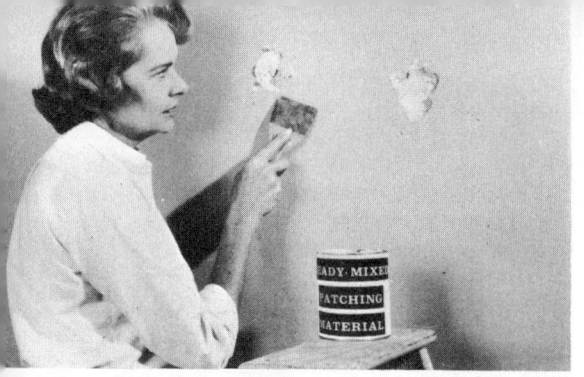

Extra time spent preparing wall surfaces will make a big difference in the final appearance of the wall covering. Loose plaster should be removed and all holes patched.

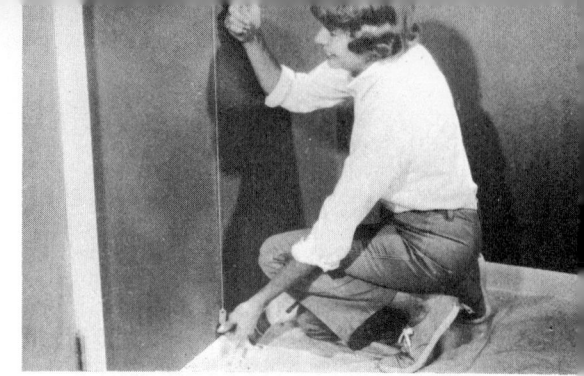

Hanging the first strip of paper properly is the most important phase of all. Use a plumb line to snap a chalk line on the wall. Use this as guide, not top or bottom of wall.

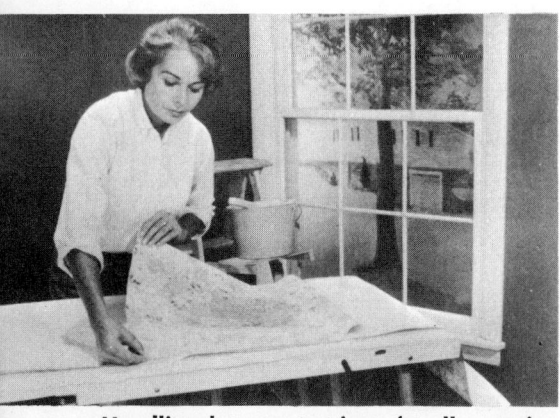

Handling long wet strips of wall covering can be tricky. Work like the "pros" and fold the wet material paste-to-paste toward center. Be very careful not to crease the fold.

To hang, unfold the top section and place on wall so it overlaps ceiling joint about 2". Tap with smoothing brush then open lower section and then gently slide into position.

A wall scraper makes an excellent guide for trimming excess material at doors, baseboards, and ceilings. For best results use a sharp razor blade. Use a holder for safety.

After working the covering with a smoothing brush, wipe all traces of paste from paper, and moldings. Do this before paste dries. Use a sponge and some clean water.

Do-it-yourself improvement ideas. Here are six small-scale projects you can do. Use fabric and wallpaper in unusual ways to dramatize a room. The sketches here highlight just a few of the many possibilities. Adapt these ideas to your personal needs.

FABRICS FOR FASHIONABLE WALL COVERINGS

Using special double-faced tape, covering walls with fabric is easy—the results fantastic

Vinyltak

Using fabric on walls is an easy way of creating exciting rooms. Fabrics with interesting colors and textures make great wall coverings, or you can take a swatch to make headboards, dividers, pictures, etc.

In the past, it was necessary to use glue on fabric to be put on a wall. At best, the job was messy and usually the results were mediocre. Air pockets, wrinkles, and uneven joints were common. All this is ancient history now, thanks to the special tapes designed for this purpose.

One high-tack double face tape (Vinyltak) makes decorating wth fabric easy as hanging a picture. One great advantage of using tape instead of glue is the fact that it does not dry out like glue, thus you can take your time in positioning and hanging the fabric.

The procedure for using the tape is quite simple. You put the tape on the fabric first, then press the fabric on the wall.

Preparation of the wall is important. The tape is designed to stick tightly and this means that it will stick to dust, loose plaster and paint just as well as it will stick to a good clean solid wall. If it does not come firmly in contact with the wall because of the dust and dirt, it is sure to loosen in a short time. The best treatment for the wall, before hanging the fabric, is to wipe the wall with a damp cloth and detergent.

Generally, the smoother the wall, the better the method will work. Rough surfaced walls such as brick, stone or textured panels, may pose problems. Very heavy fabrics should be avoided; however, fairly heavy fabrics have been used with success by adding extra strips of tape down the middle of each fabric panel.

Spread the fabric on the floor and apply tape about ¼" from the edge on all four sides. Do not remove the backing from the tape. Fabric should be free of rough edges.

Starting at the top, remove about 12" of backing from tape, and firmly press fabric into place. In order to stick well, pressure-sensitive tape should be applied firmly.

Remove the tape's backing about 12" at a time, pulling toward you as you remove it. Secure that part of the fabric and repeat the procedure. Don't do too much at one time.

The process is repeated for the opposite side. Pull the fabric taut as you go to eliminate air pockets. Do not overdo as the results could be just as bad as the air pockets.

Children's favorite Walt Disney characters are well represented in this colorful wall covering. Heavy gauge 18" wide material can take plenty abuse, will not scuff and is washable. Great for play area.

29

SKIN FOR A DULL DOOR

Make an old door look like new

You can easily renew an old door by giving it a facelift using one of the new decorator vinyl coverings. Extra-wide pre-cut vinyl (37") can be used for doors measuring 36" wide or less. The average door in the home is 30" wide.

Woodgrain vinyl and matching trim tape is available as a kit. Width is 37" and will cover a 36" door with ½" overlap on all sides. If necessary, trim so width is 1" wider than door.

The vinyl is available in various woodgrains from knotty pine to the exotic walnut and teak. The patterns are so realistic, it is hard to tell the difference between the vinyl and real wood.

Because doors are subject to much abuse, they become unsightly in a short time, especially if there are children in the home. Paint and varnish are easily scuffed, but the vinyls have abrasion-resistant coatings which will stand up much better and take more abuse.

To cover a door, remove it from the hinges and place on a pair of sawhorses. Remove all hardware and proceed as outlined in the photos.

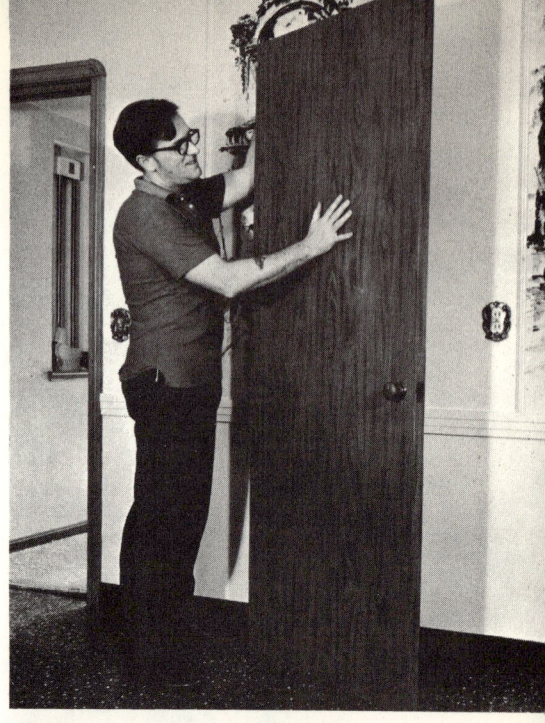

All photos courtesy Morgan Adhesive Co.

Door to be covered should be removed from hinges. Lay flat between a pair of chairs or saw horses. Hollow door is light and can be handled easily by one man.

Sand down any rough spots and if varnish or paint is chipped or cracked, be sure to remedy before next step. Deep cracks or gouges should then be filled with spackle.

After trimming skin to size and just before applying, dampen surface of door with sponge dipped in solution of soapy water. (½ teaspoon detergent to 1 gallon water.)

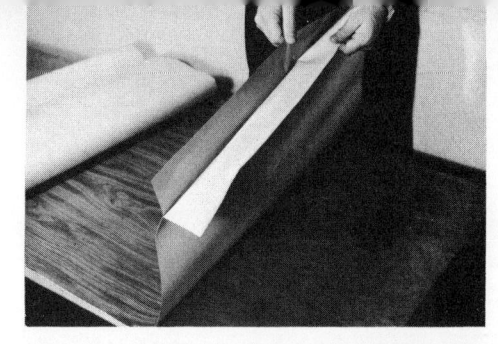

Protective backing paper is carefully peeled down 2" from top of vinyl sheet. Be sure hands are clean when handling the adhesive side of vinyl. Keep adhesive from touching.

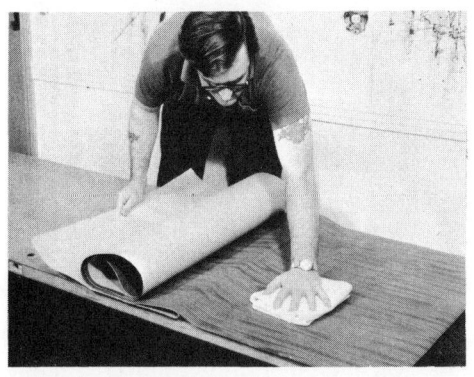

Gently and steadily release backing paper while smoothing vinyl to door surface. Use a terry cloth pad and stroke from center toward edges. Work out all air pockets.

After vinyl has been applied to door surface and the ½" overlap wrapped around edges, apply matching trim tape to conceal the edge wrap. Keep trim centered on edge.

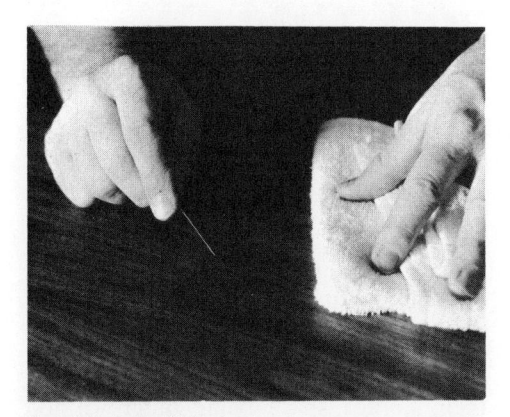

Should air bubbles appear due to air pockets, prick bubble with a pin to release air and complete bond of adhesive to door surface. The pin holes will not be visible.

Before replacing hardware, use a razor blade or sharp knife to cut hole for shaft and latch mortise. Do likewise for the door hinges. Don't cut the holes too big though.

31

Western Wood Prod. Association

Hide-away study was built into a standard closet. Shelves of western pine on side wall leave top of desk free. Drawers below are set to clear the open bi-fold louvered doors.

STRETCH THAT STORAGE SPACE

Make better use of space you have or cleverly create new storage

Rich or poor, young or old, we all tend to accumulate more and more possessions as time goes on. Some purely personal, some recreational, some decorative, some useful and necessary in the general day to day living. If all these belongings were piled high in the center of our living quarters, what a huge and ugly mountain we would have to face each day.

But man's creativity has enabled him to sort out and store away these items, each group in its own particular place, such as closets, shelves, drawers, bookcases, etc. However, most homes, especially young families and households, find their storage space being outgrown too much and too soon. The result is untidiness such as toys lying in the middle of the floor or shoved under a bed, groceries left on a counter or table, clothes thrown

This unsightly mess is probably typical in many homes. Open shelves in basement seem to invite household items, some usable and some not. Clothing stored here, unprotected, is more susceptible to moths.

Same area converted into a fine cedar-lined closet which repels moths, smells refreshing and "breathes" luxury. Fragrant aromatic red cedar is unpleasant to moths and paralyzes larvae. The entire closet is cedar.

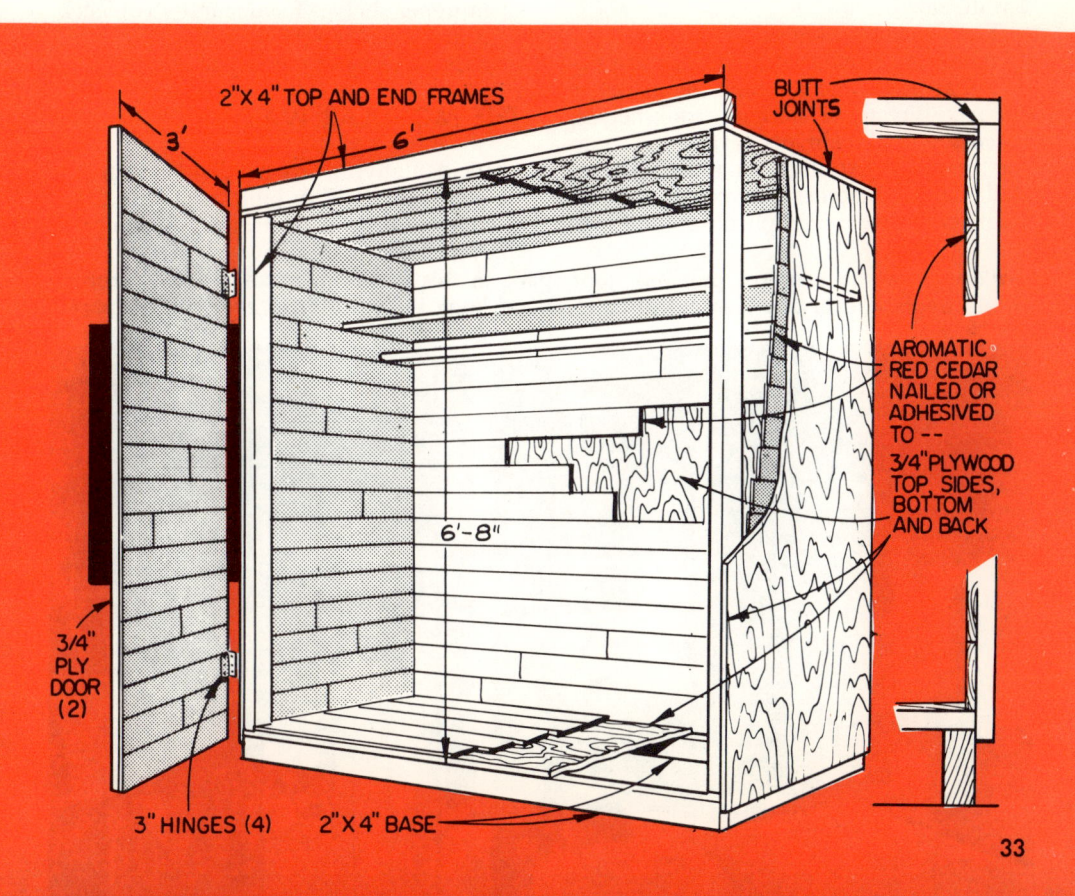

2"x 4" TOP AND END FRAMES

3'

6'

BUTT JOINTS

AROMATIC RED CEDAR NAILED OR ADHESIVED TO —

3/4" PLYWOOD TOP, SIDES, BOTTOM AND BACK

6'-8"

3/4" PLY DOOR (2)

3" HINGES (4)

2"X 4" BASE

33

Western Wood Prod. Association

Plenty of storage for books on this wall and under window. Shelving is made of ponderosa pine and easily constructed. Butt joints used throughout. Back panels are ¼"-plywood.

over a chair or bed, tools resting against a wall, etc.

The list seems endless.

When you reach that point, or even before that, it is time to think about better storage. Buying or making bookshelves, hutches, and file cabinets, if you have room for them, are excellent for more storage. Built-ins are another source. Room dividers can serve a dual purpose; the lower shelves or compartments for storage, and open upper shelves for decorative objects. The divider thus serves as a storage unit besides dividing two living areas.

THE MODULAR WAY

Incidentally, a room divider can be bought readymade or built from scratch by a competent do-it-yourselfer. A compro-

Shallow closets to preserve precious floor space in this bedroom make use of mirrored bi-fold doors. Clever arrangement of hangers and linen shelves utilizes every bit of space.
U. S. Plywood

Masonite Corp.

Thin pull-out shelves spaced a few inches apart solve the storage problem in this porch closet. Grooves sawn in the uprights receive pegboard shelves. It's repeated below.

Western Wood Prod. Association

This laundry center combines elegance and practicality. Cabinets above the appliances store necessary washing supplies. Bulky soap cartons are stored in cabinet below.

mise for the amateur do-it-yourselfer is to buy the cabinets ready-made, as many units as needed, and to mount them on walls as buffets, or assemble them together as free-standing room dividers. The ready-made modular cabinets come in various sizes and can be fit in anywhere in kitchen, bath, hall, dining room, etc. The tops of these cabinets may be covered with slate, ceramic tile, vinyl, etc.

Amerock

SHELVES DO IT

Closets can be a source of more storage. Shelves can be installed at the top of a closet to make it possible to utilize the normally wasted space. Pegboards on a wall other than the workshop will help to organize any area whether it be the toolshed, garage, or even laundry room. Hang a pegboard on the back of a closet door and you'll have at least 16 square feet of additional space.

For small-item storage, consider building or buying back-of-door shelves for closet doors in almost any room in the house—the pantry, the kitchen, laundry room, clothes closets, etc. The ready-made shelves are easily installed. There are also available easily installed drawer units and rotating shelves to make better use of cabinet space.

Off-season clothing storage is always a problem. If you build a cedar lined closet, you will have solved two problems. The fragrant aromatic red cedar will repel moths and it paralyzes the larvae. A free-

Adjustable shelves on door of this home office cabinet make good use of space. Units can also be used in the shop for storing small parts. Standards are screwed on.

35

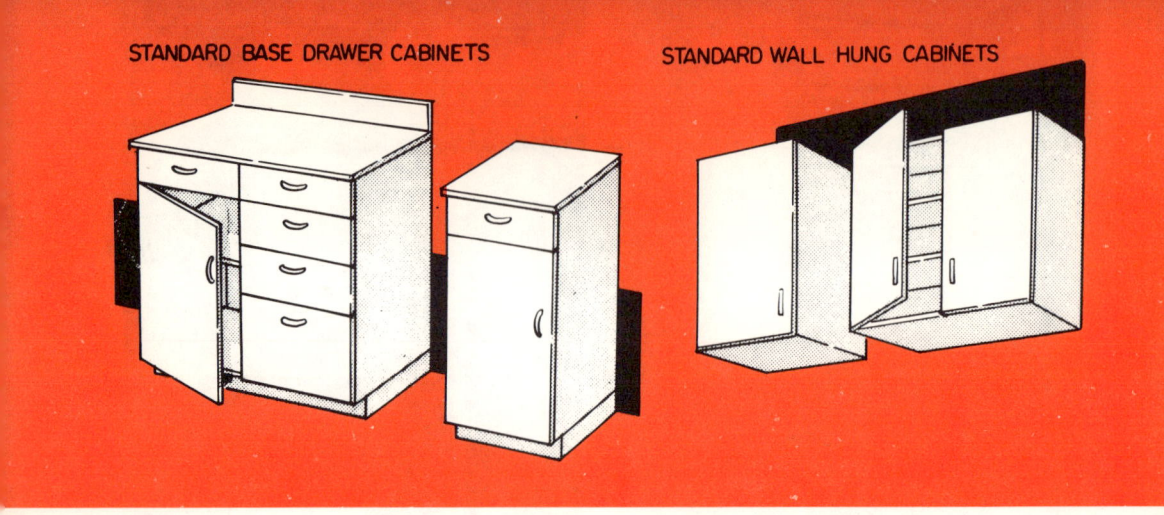

STANDARD BASE DRAWER CABINETS   **STANDARD WALL HUNG CABINETS**

standing closet may be built to stand in the basement or attic. Other possibilities are a cedar lined storage wall in the bedroom or even a room divider.

Red cedar for lining closets comes in strip form ⅜″ thick and 2″ to 4″ wide. Lengths vary from 2′ to 8′. The strips are tongue-and-grooved along the edges and ends. The drawing shows how to build a free-standing unit.

A novel plan for adding a so-called "Elbow Room" is available from the Western Wood Products Assoc., Dept. 545-46P, Yeon Bldg., Portland, Oregon, 97204, for only 25 cents in coin. This Elbow Room is a small wood-paneled 6 x 8 ft. addition to a home that utilizes existing power and heat facilities. It can be utilized as a sewing or hobby room, a bunkroom, a home office, etc. Generally the costs average $600. The room is built on a concrete slab and has either a shed or gable roof. The exterior is finished with siding to complement the existing home. This room may be just what you are looking for.

Messy garage clutter disappears on these handy storage shelves. The perforated hardboard stores tall or bulky items. Bi-fold doors are ideal for small, crowded garage.
Georgia-Pacific

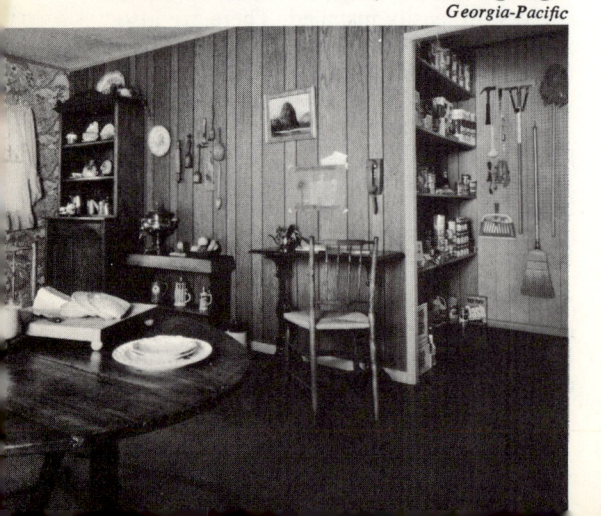

This handy pantry-broom closet is just a step away from the food preparation area. The practical storage panel and open shelves keep everything readily accessible.
Georgia-Pacific

Georgia-Pacific

Storage for seasonal items can pose a problem. Here, unused attic area was paneled horizontally and put to good use. End wall was fitted with perforated hardboard to hold items.

Metal or wood bi-fold doors are excellent for closing off a storage area. They are available in many sizes and are easy to install. Overhead track eliminates any obstruction.

Give the lady of the house more elbow room for her sewing center. Brightly colored walls keep light level high, and smooth flooring makes for easier cleanup of scraps.

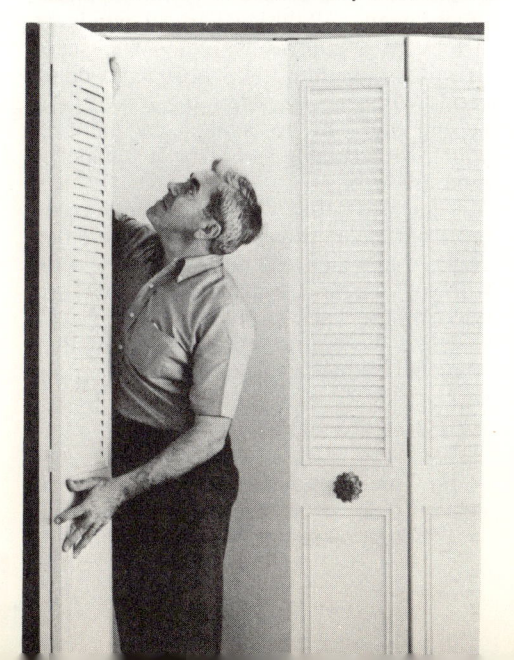

37

Light-colored walls and ceiling make this room appear spacious and airy. Dark beams and woodwork contrast nicely with walls. Tweed patterned flooring blends in with room decor.

PAINTS AND PAINTING

Fast, economical and improved, paints are now even easier to use

The oldest, the quickest, and usually the most economical way to redo interior walls is by the use of paint. New innovations have greatly improved this field. Exciting new decorator colors are on the market.

Qualities of paints have improved. Just a few years ago, two coats of a water soluble paint were required to cover a wall and there was little choice regarding the surface—flat, or flatter!

Thanks to modern technology, water base paints are now available in varying grades of flat, eggshell and even gloss. They cover better and they are easier to use. Most paints are odorless, quick-drying, and economically priced.

Painting will not only improve the appearance of your room, but a light color will make a small room appear larger and a dark color will make a large room appear much smaller. Painting vertical bands or stripes of a contrasting color will seem to raise the ceiling, and horizontal color bands will seem to lower the ceiling. An accent wall can be created, by painting your own freehand mural or psychedelic, mod art work.

Remember, that when you select a color for a particular room, the 2" square color chips from which you make your selection will not appear the same when they are covering the walls of a large room. Try to visualize the entire wall or room in that color before making your choice.

BRUSH OR ROLLER?

For most applications, the roller is generally used for painting interiors. It is

38

You can keep it simple or go ultramodern with a super-graphic paint job like the zigzag stripe pattern shown here. Masking tape can be used to outline the design that you choose.

Prepare work by filling nail holes and dents then apply base coat. Unfinished wood requires two coats. Most base coats are latex and recoating can usually be done quickly.

Antiquing furniture is one way to decorate your home. You can finish a piece of furniture or even woodwork on the walls, using prepared kits with everything you need.

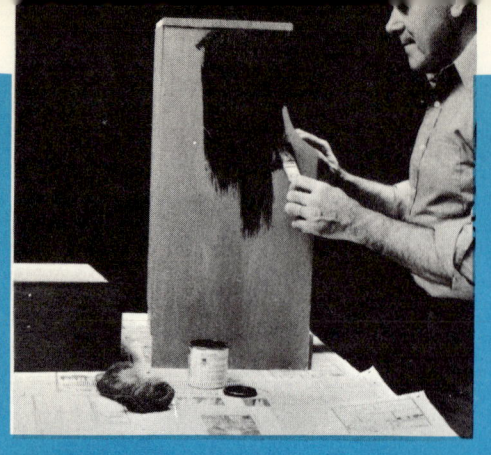

Glaze coat is the secret of antiquing. Apply liberally with brush or cloth and cover completely. Before it starts to set, it must be wiped so only streaks will show.

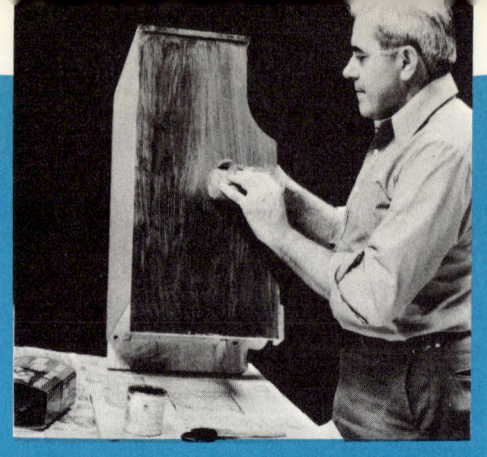

Almost anything can be used in the final wiping operation, such as paper towelling or a dry brush or fine steel wool. Graining must be done with the length of the piece.

so easy to use and the results are professional. This does not mean that brushes are passe. Edges and corners must still be painted with a brush. Likewise glossy paints should be applied with brushes. Rollers tend to leave a textured surface. The type of roller used depends on the surface to be painted. Rough textured surfaces are best done with a long-napped roller. Flat smooth surfaces call for short bristled rollers. Your paint dealer can advise you here.

ANTIQUING

In addition to coating walls and ceilings, paints are widely used in decorating accessories. Drab looking pieces of furniture can be brightly painted to liven up a room. Special effects such as antiquing can alter a piece completely. Antiquing is widely used on unpainted furniture, chests, doors, windows, bric-a-brac, etc.

The technique is not difficult to master. A base color is given a glaze coat which is then wiped off in such a manner as to give the effect of an old antique finish. The glaze sticks into cracks and crevices as well as corners for a very pleasing effect.

Ready-to-use antiquing kits are available at all paint and department stores. Some kits consist of the undercoater and glaze, while others offer a complete package including brushes, steel wool, cloth, sander and the necessary coatings. Many color combinations are offered and most displays feature finished samples so that you will know beforehand exactly what the finished pieces will look like.

Some tricks used in antiquing are distressing, shading and splatter. Distressing is done in any number of ways: striking the piece with chains, awls, screwdriver points, etc. The edges can be "worn" by rounding them off with a spokeshave or sandpaper. A belt sander will work well but use care as it "cuts" fast.

● Shading is done by using colors in oil. These come in tubes. For wood tones use the earth colors, raw sienna and raw umber. For painted furniture choose a color to match the piece. Mix a small amount of raw sienna and raw umber for the wood tones. Use a cloth to apply the color as is without thinning, to the edges of the piece. Wipe with a clean cloth working out from the center. The color should blend with the heavier deposit near the edges. Oils dry slow so you have time to experiment to achieve the desired results.

● Splatter is done by flicking dark spots onto the work using a stiff brush. An old toothbrush works fine. Take a small amount of raw umber and thin with turpentine. Do not overthin. Just thin enough so it can be flicked from the brush. Run your fingernail over the bristles and let the spray strike the work.

● After the finishing is completed and the undercoats have dried sufficiently, coat the work with a clear coating of varnish or lacquer.

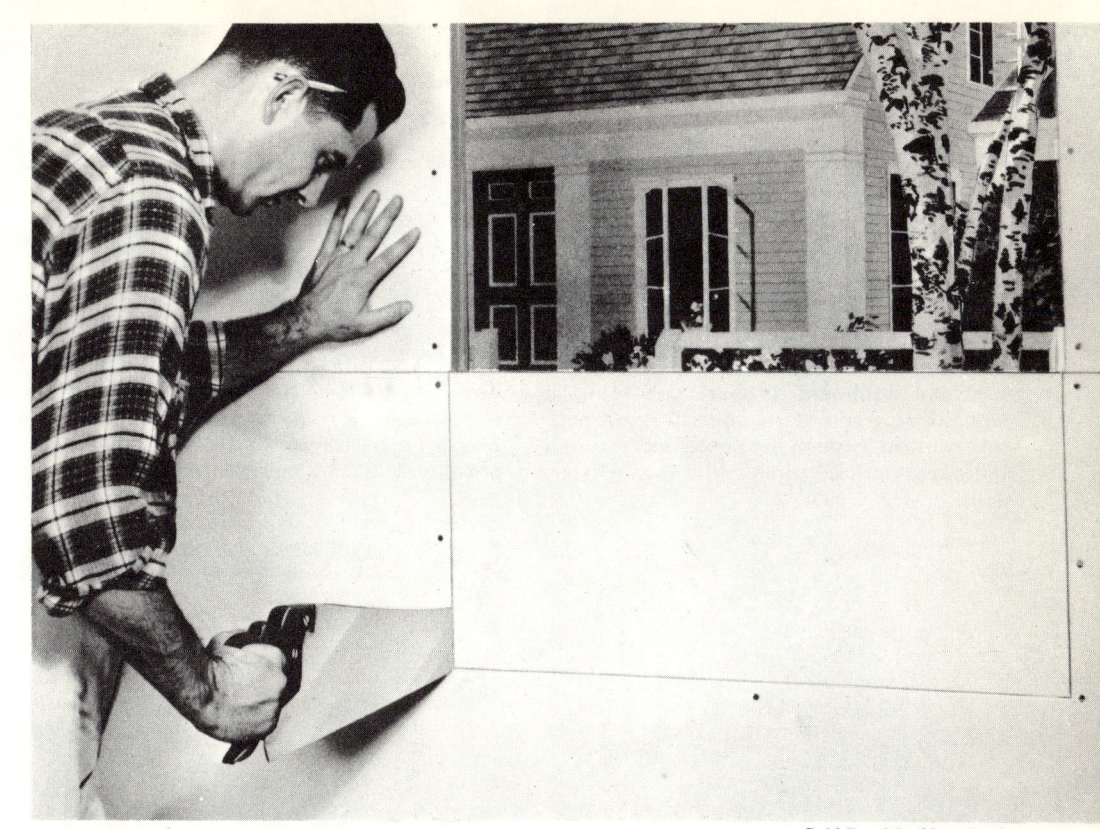

Gold Bond Building Prod.

Dry wall is one of the most economical materials that can be used in remodeling. Panels are available in varying lengths and they can be installed by using common, everyday tools.

INSTALLING WALLBOARD

Know these very important fundamentals before tackling a dry-wall

Many home improvement projects call for the installation of a dry-wall. This is usually sheetrock which is a plaster core laminated on both sides with a hard surfacing. This material is also known as plasterboard or gypsum wallboard. The sheets are available 48" wide and from 6-to-12 ft. long in one foot increments. The installation is not difficult and the tool requirements are nil. *You will need the following:* hammer, saw, straight edge, 6" broad knife, utility knife, joint compound, and perforated tape.

Gypsum wallboard takes paint or wallpaper easily and if installed properly the joints will be invisible. The sequence photos show a typical installation. Ready-mixed joint compound has the proper consistency so that taping of joints is greatly simplified.

Some tips to remember when working with wallboard are as follows: Sink the nailheads slightly and place two nails at each location instead of the usual one. This will keep nail "popping" to a minimum. Always begin nailing from the center out. Apply at least two coats of bedding compound over joints.

Gypsum wallboard is best cut using a straight edge and utility knife. It is not necessary to cut through the board, just through the paper surface and slightly into plaster.

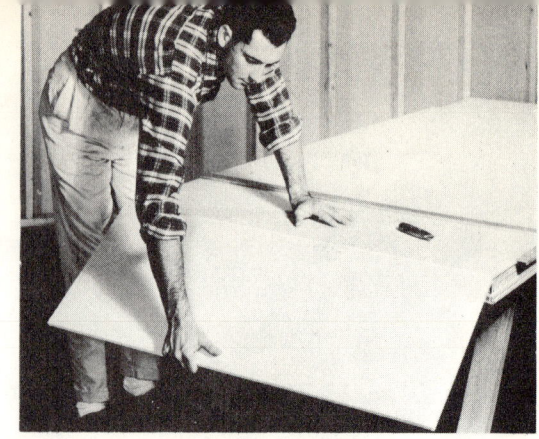

The board will break cleanly if it is snapped over a solid support. A quick action produces best results. Backing sheet will not separate, but must be cut from back.

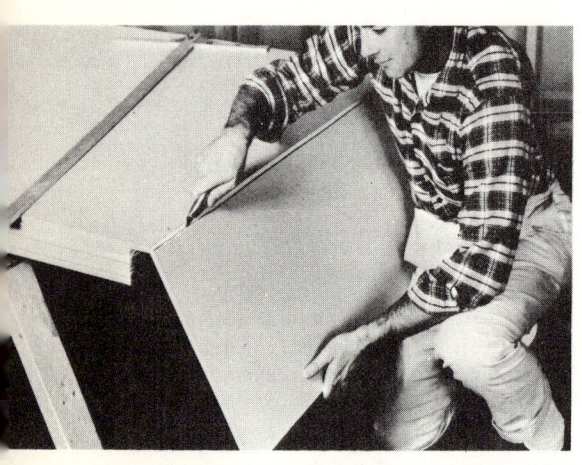

To cut through the backing, support the overhang and cut through as shown. Cutouts for electric boxes are scored then knocked out with a hammer or keyhole saw.

Installation should always start at the ceiling. Boards are mounted at right angles to joists. Temporary brace made with 2 x 4 lumber supports weight of board easily.

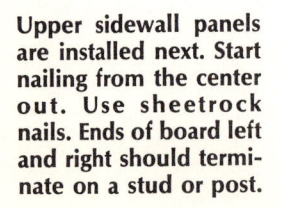

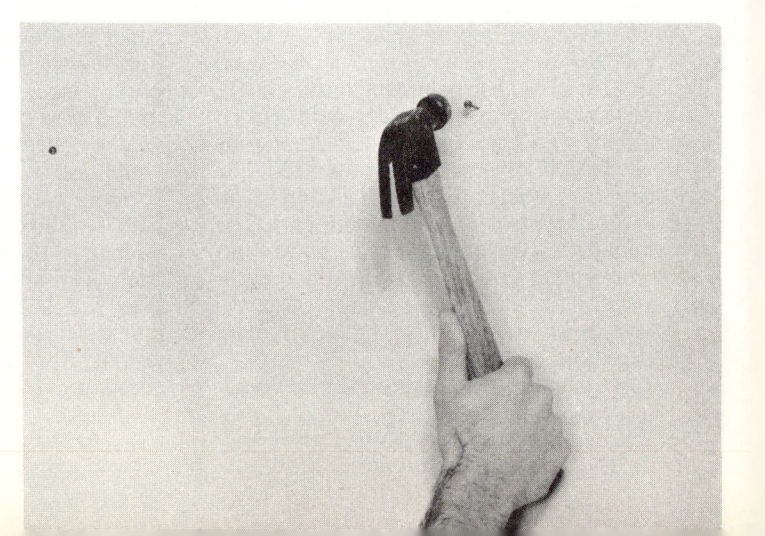

Upper sidewall panels are installed next. Start nailing from the center out. Use sheetrock nails. Ends of board left and right should terminate on a stud or post.

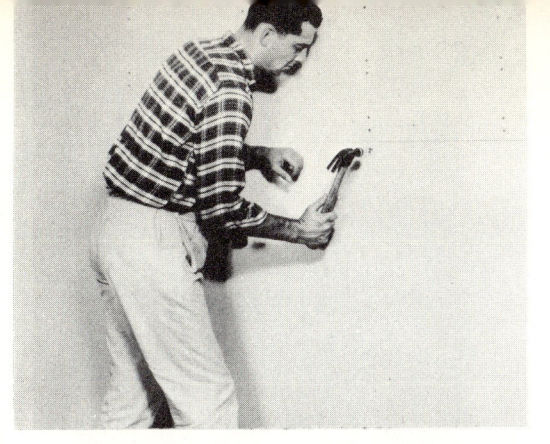

Lower sidewall panel is held snugly against upper panel while nailing—simple foot-operated lever holds them in place. Double nailing will keep the popping to minimum.

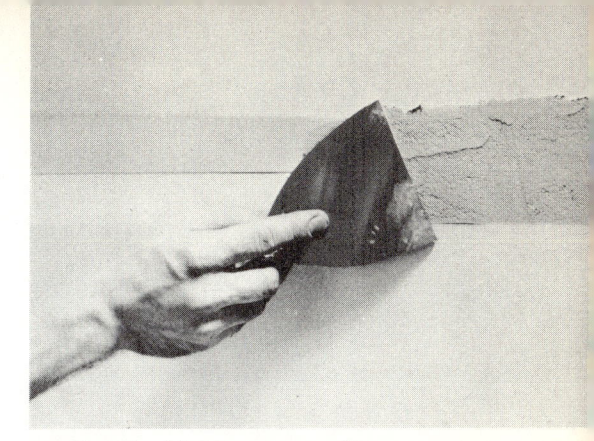

Ready-mixed joint compound is easy to use. Material has consistency of heavy cream and is applied with broad knife. Channel between the wallboard edges is filled.

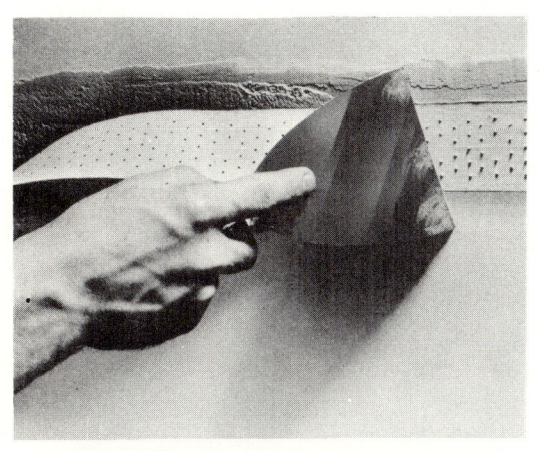

Perforated tape is embedded into the compound directly over the joint. Smooth the compound around and over the tape to level the surface. Spot nail heads with it.

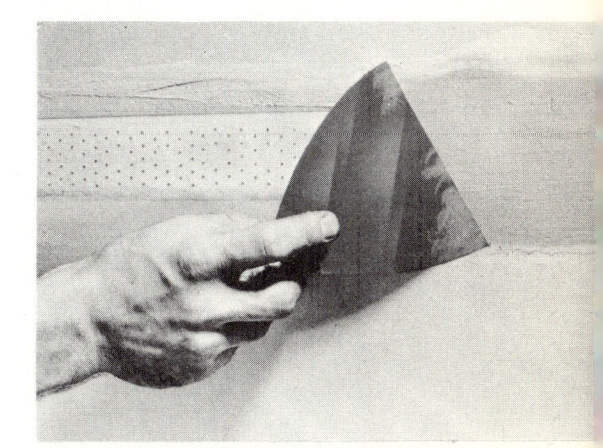

A second coat of bedding compound is applied after first coat has dried for at least 24 hours. Apply thinly and feather out 3" to 4" on each side of joint. Allow to dry 24 hours.

Final coat is applied very thinly and feathered out about 8" to 10" on each side of channel. Finish by sanding cement smooth. Avoid heavy pressure which may scuff the surface.

43

Majestic Co.

This attractive wall-hung fireplace is gas fired. It comes in a variety of decorator colors and has a lighted log. Woodburning units are also available. Both can be easily installed.

FACTORY-BUILT, WALL-HUNG FIREPLACE

Installs fast without masonry

A new prefabricated woodburning (or gas fired) fireplace which does not require masonry foundation, framing or finishing, is now available to homeowners. Manufactured by the Majestic Co., the unit features triple wall construction which totally insulate them. The fireplace can be mounted directly against any wall on any floor material and in any location.

The units are designed to accommodate ceilings in the 7-to-8 ft. range.

Venting is by standard 9" chimney components. Various chimney tops are available to complete the vent system of the installation.

This striking combination fireplace-room divider was built by a homeowner in his spare time. Original room had an "L" shaped wall which has been replaced by the fireplace.

COMBINATION ROOM DIVIDER-FIREPLACE

Build it in your spare time

With the accent turning toward luxury these days, even the joys of a fireplace can take on a versatile, new meaning. No longer used only to supply heat, that warming glow can now be transformed and beautifully appointed to serve as a divider for otherwise cool or rambling rooms. And with the selection of a factory-built, quality engineered fireplace, today's average homeowner can even tackle the installa-

45

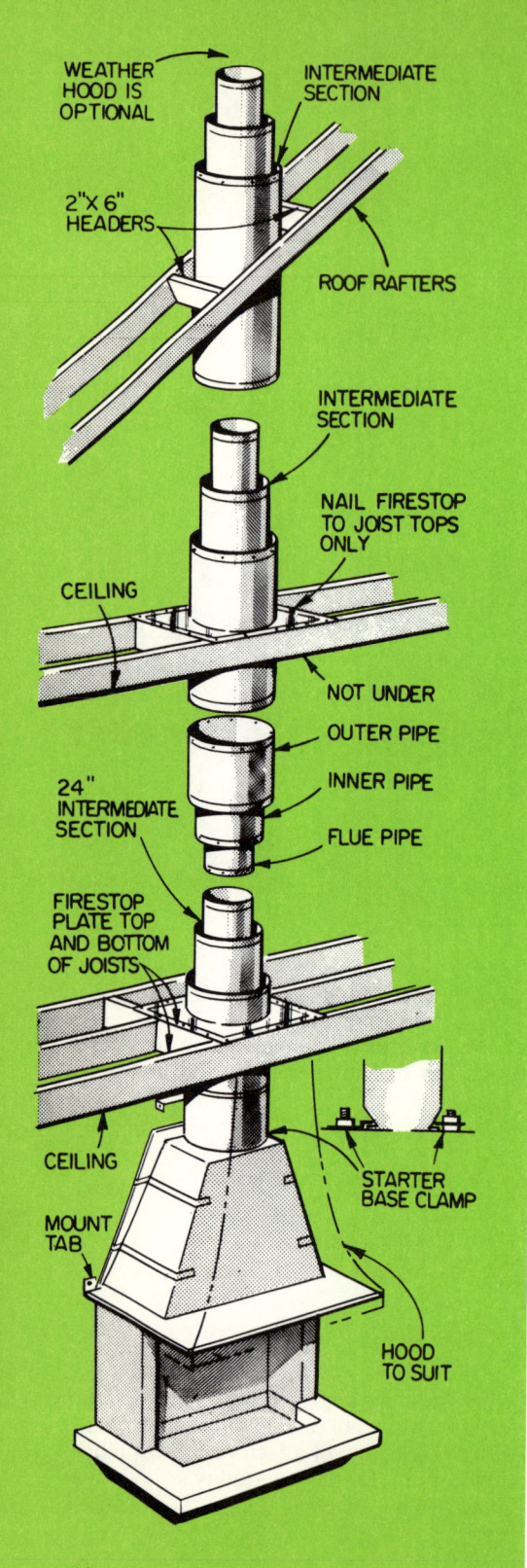

This electric fireplace is as easy to install as hanging a picture. Plugged into any wall outlet the log set flickers realistically. For additional heat heater unit is available.

Majestic Co.

Prefabricated all-metal fireplaces are supplied with no masonry required. The exterior facing is finished to suit individual taste. As shown in sketch, chimney is in 3 sections.

46

Photo shows how room appeared before transformation. Because of the weight of brick and mortar, an installation of this type is recommended only over a slab floor.

All metal fireplace doesn't look too attractive at this stage. Note how base is shimmed to bring floor of firebox to desired height. Floor may slope but firebox must be level.

tion himself, in his spare time. The room scenes pictured here are typical examples.

Note the room prior to fireplace installation. The living and dining areas were both rolled into one. A simple "L" shaped wall served to divide the room, but actually did not allow for the secluded "cozy" atmosphere intended. By placing the fireplace in the center of the room and then taking up otherwise unused floor space to add a bar extending to the wall, you can see two rooms taking on their own character and a new air of formality taking hold.

READY-MADE FIREPLACES

By starting with a pre-built steel unit, this homeowner was able to accomplish much of the installation on his own and could then select whatever motif he desired. Here, finishing touches of moss green woodgrained panels to match the decorations of the dining room were complemented by the rugged looking "clinker" brick to also add an unusual contrast to the walnut paneling in the now more exciting living room.

Also by using a pre-built unit, the room will be more comfortable year-round. When the damper is closed, no air will escape from the room during the summer to upset the air conditioning, and during the winter, heat is provided and a minimum of this warmed air is drawn from the room.

Venting was achieved by running the all-metal flue up through the ceiling into the second floor, and out through the roof. With careful planning, the flue was positioned to be concealed in an existing upstairs closet, thus minimizing construction and consumption of usable room space while providing very efficient handling of this critical part of the fireplace operation.

This modern pre-engineered fireplace was also more attractive from a safety angle. Designed for zero clearance to combustibles, this unit could be safely placed in any position in the room, and likewise located so that the flue would extend through an upstairs closet and thus be conveniently concealed. Heavy-duty steel construction tightly sealed at every joint accounts for maximum efficiency.

To enhance the setting even more, a bar was added, accessible to the dining area, with smooth dark walnut paneling added facing the living room, extending from the rugged brick fireplace side to the now enticing wall. A simulated slate top of formica was added to the bar to complete the magical transition. All of this excitement has been easily made possible for this homeowner, and along with it come the long-lasting joys of having his own real wood-burning fireplace.

The results were remarkable. With a little ingenuity and a bit of hard work, one plain cold room has been transformed into two charming, cozy ones.

Armstrong Cork Co. photo
No-wax floors can help spare the housewife unnecessary drudgery. Flooring needs only occasional damp mopping to keep it clean, shines without wax. Waxes won't even stick.

FOCUS ON FLOORS

Basic facts you'll need to find the right floor covering for you

Floor coverings are of primary importance in any extensive room remodeling. They should harmonize and blend tastefully with all other furnishings and wall decor. They may be bold in color and pattern and dominant, yet they must not distract or clash with the general theme or mood of the room in which used.

There is an almost infinite variety of flooring material available today. Your selection should be based not only on appearance, but also on the ease of installation, maintenance, durability, and area to be covered. Some of the materials from which to choose are: carpeting, wood, cork, resilient coverings, ceramic tiles, stone, brick, seamless plastics, and just plain paint.

WOOD FLOORS

Wood floors may be left natural with a clear finish or they may be stained or bleached to enhance the grain and bring out the beauty of the wood. Hardwood floors are available in strips or blocks. Blocks come in many patterns, both unfinished and prefinished.

48

QUALITIES OF RESILIENT FLOOR TILES

Type of Tile	Grease-Resistance	On Concrete	Foot Comfort	Easy-Care	Durability	Static Load Resistance	Quiet Walking	Relative Cost
Pure vinyl	Excellent	Excellent	Very good	Excellent	Excellent	Excellent	Very good	Med. to very high
Vinyl asbestos	Excellent	Very good	Good	Good	Good	Fair	Good	Medium
Rubber	Fair	Good	Excellent	Good	Excellent	Excellent	Very good	High
Unsealed cork	Poor	Poor	Excellent	Poor	Good	Good	Excellent	Med. to high
Linoleum	Very good	Poor	Poor	Good	Fair	Good	Very good	Medium
Asphalt	Poor	Good	Fair	Poor	Poor	Poor	Fair	Low

FLOOR COVERINGS YOU CAN USE

Material	Thickness	Unit Size	Features	Relative Cost
Resilient tile, sheet	1/16" to 1/8"	9" x 9" to 12" x 12" and rolls	Large selection of colors, patterns, materials. Easy to fit, install. Some wear well. Most are reasonably easy to care for.	Low to high
Wood-strip	5/16" to 25/32"	Boards 1½" to 8" wide	Beauty and solidity of wood flooring. Comes prefinished. Easy to lay and wears well. Hardwoods and softwoods, antique and modern styles.	Medium to high
Wood-block	5/16" to 1/2"	6½" square to 9½" square	Same as above. Makes a quality feature in any home. Is laid by nailing or in mastic over old floor or subfloor.	Medium
Rigid tile	1/4" to 1/2"	3" x 6" to 12" x 12"	Quarry and slate tiles are most suited for striking beauty and long wear in entries, living rooms, kitchens.	High
Carpet-tile	Varies	12" x 12"	This is the only kind of carpeting you can install yourself and get the beauty, quiet and luxury of carpeting.	Medium
Seamless	3 coats	Quart	Goes on like paint. Color flakes are available in many colors. Creates a tough, easy-to-care-for floor for kitchens, baths, laundries. Outdoors too.	Medium

49

Modern flooring materials are economical, go down quick and easy. This floor was installed in a few hours without messy adhesives. Tiles have sticky back and are simply pressed on.

Strip flooring must be nailed and so the sub-floor must be of wood or other nailable material. Blocks may be nailed or set in mastic. Some block flooring is available pre-glued. The protective backing is merely peeled off to expose the glued surface, and the blocks are then simply pressed into place. The blocks and strips are tongue and grooved.

RESILIENT MATERIALS

Resilient floor coverings are great do-it-yourself materials. A large variety of styles and colors are available. They now come also with pressure-sensitive adhesives on the back, eliminating the need for spreading cement during installation.

These tiles have a latex type adhesive which will bond to any smooth surface floor. The tiles will hold firmly to existing tiles, linoleum, and sheet vinyl. Floors must however be spotless and free of all dirt, wax and grease. Sheet materials are best left to the professional installer.

CONVENTIONAL TILES

Conventional tiles are installed after the floor has been properly prepared. All chips and cracks must be filled and low spots levelled in concrete floors. Mastic is then spread by trowel, brush or roller. Wood floors must be lined with felt to keep the joints in the floor from showing through the new tiles. Sub-floors which are in poor shape should be underlayed with ¼" hardboard made expressly for the purpose. The chart printed below lists the various types of flooring available and also the relative costs.

Even a child can install this tile. It's almost impossible to make a mistake. If improperly placed, the tile can be repositioned. Note that it is installed on a previously tiled floor.

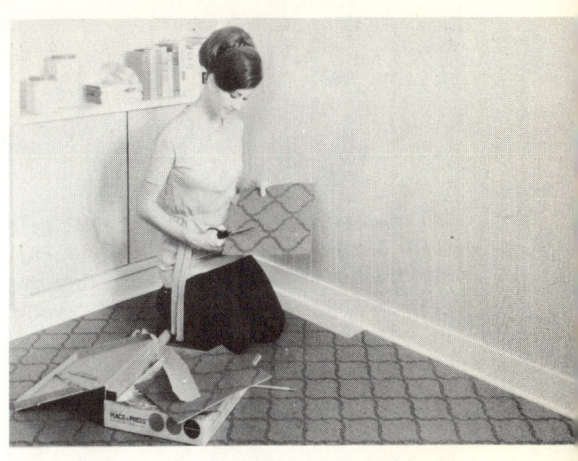

Border tiles for the perimeter of the room can be cut with ordinary household shears or razor blade. The protective backing paper is left on tile until ready to be installed.

FLOOR COVERINGS YOU CAN USE

Material	Thickness	Unit Size	Feature	Relative Cost
Resilient tile, sheet	1/6" to 1/8"	9" x 9" to 12" x 12" and rolls	Large selection of colors, patterns, materials. Easy to fit, install. Some wear well. Most are reasonably easy to care for.	Low to high
Wood-strip	5/16" to 25/32"	Boards 1½" to 8" wide	Beauty and solidity of wood flooring. Comes prefinished. Easy to lay and wears well. Hardwoods and softwoods, antique and modern styles.	Medium to high
Wood-block	5/16" to 1/2"	6½" square to 9½" square	Same as above. Makes a quality feature in any home. Is laid by nailing or in mastic over old floor or subfloor.	Medium
Rigid tile	1/4" to 1/2"	3" x 6" to 12" x 12"	Quarry and slate tiles are most suited for striking beauty and long wear in entries, living rooms, kitchens.	High
Carpet-tile	Varies	12" x 12"	This is the only kind of carpeting you can install yourself and get the beauty, quiet and luxury of carpeting.	Medium
Seamless	3 coats	Quart	Goes on like paint. Color flakes are available in many colors. Creates a tough, easy-to-care-for floor for kitchens, baths, laundries. Outdoors too.	Medium

51

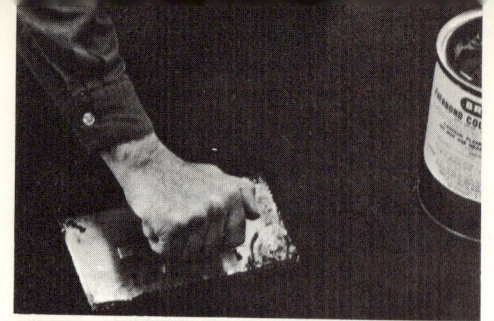

Mastic is spread onto floor with notched trowel. Do several square feet at a time and apply sparingly. Smooth it out evenly.

POURED FLOORS

Poured floors are becoming quite popular. These are the so-called seamless floors. They are actually poured wet onto the floor, then spread evenly with a trowel. Colorful chips may be imbedded before the liquid hardens to form many interesting patterns. The material dries into a very tough and seamless floor which will give many years of service.

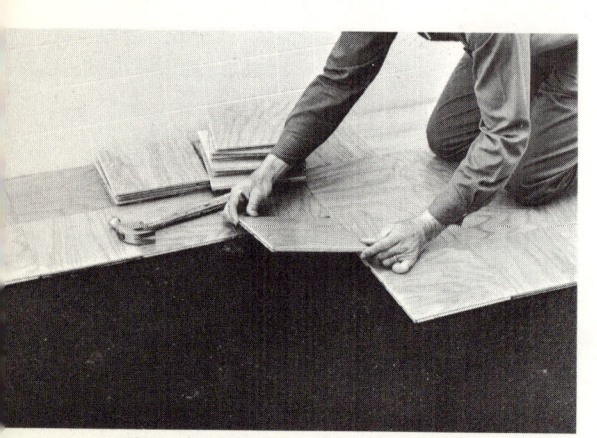

Tiles are ideally suited for the do-it-yourselfer. Floor must be flat and free of defects. Apply mastic with notched trowel and set.

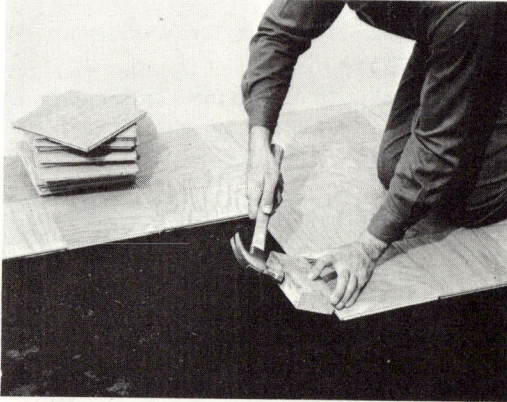

A mallet and block of wood are used to set the tiles. The entire surface must be covered to insure the best possible adhesion.

Preassembled ornamental borders are ⅜" thick and 7" wide. Corner blocks are 5¼" square and border sections are 28" long. Handy units are furnished paperfaced.

Bangkok Ind.

Double herringbone patterned hardwood floor is elegant and durable. Available in unit strips ⅜" x 12" for mastic installation. Achieve double herringbone with 2 strips.

Bangkok Ind.

Armstrong's Epilogue do-it-yourself shag carpet combines easy installation and luxurious appearance at moderate cost. Latex backing permits loose-lay, tape or adhesive installation.

DO-IT-YOURSELF CARPETING

Do-it-yourself carpeting is a boon to the remodeling homeowner. Moderately priced, it is available both in 12" square tiles and in 6 ft. and 12 ft. wide rolls. The tiles are adhesive-backed and the roll material is foam-backed.

The carpet tiles come in various colors which may be combined to form checkerboard or other patterns for unusual effects. They can be used on almost any clean flat surface. Wood and cement floors should be treated first with a sealer before laying the tiles.

The roll carpeting is foam-backed and features pre-cut factory edges which assures perfect fitting of edges to hide seams.

Few tools are required for installation. A straight edge, marking pen and shears are all you need. Section around door has been folded back and then marked with a pen.

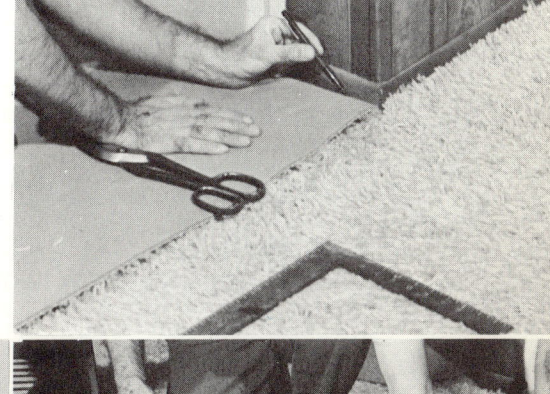

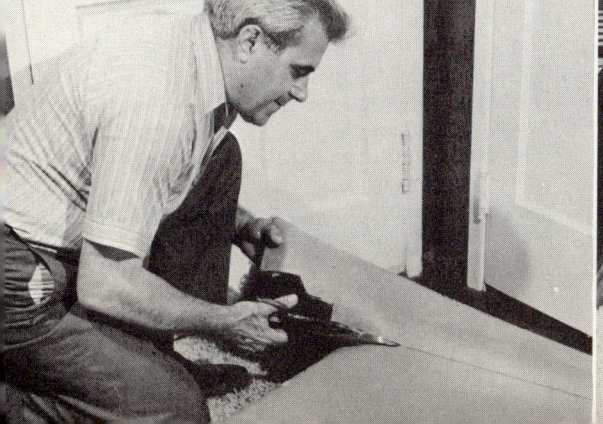

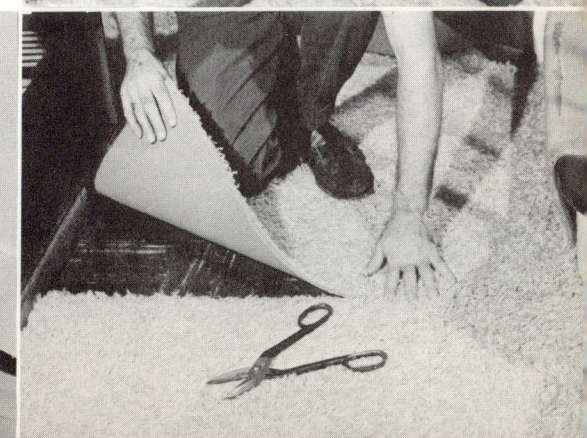

American Olean Tile Co.

Ceramic tile's timeless beauty is shown here in all its glory. The low-relief tiles are 12" x 12" and can be used on floors and walls. Tiles are frostproof, wear and impact resistant.

CERAMIC TILES

Ceramic tiles are an excellent floor covering material. At one time, they were used mostly in bathrooms, but this is no longer true. Now any room in the home can be tiled, even family and workrooms.

The tiles are used not only for floors and walls, they can be used for countertops, fireplaces, and even for furniture. Ceramic tiles are permanent, hard-wearing, and easy to clean. For the artistic minded, ceramic mosaic murals offer unlimited possibilities.

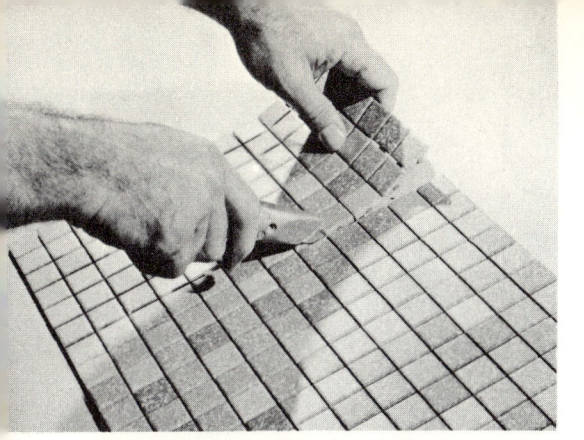

Preassembled mosaic tiles come in 2-foot by one-foot sheets. Sheets hold tiles in permanent alignment with special adhesive. Tiles can be separated with knife for fitting.

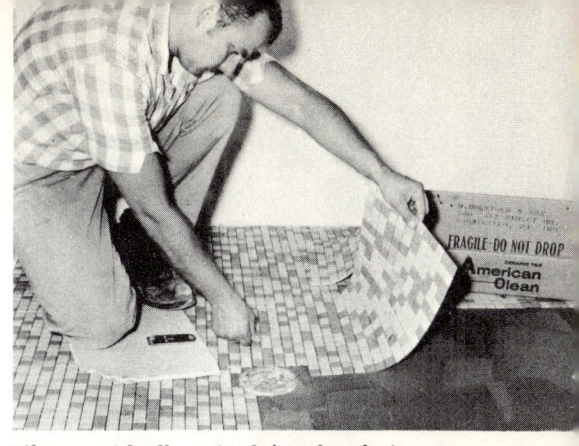

Tiles are ideally suited for the do-it-yourselfer. Floor must be flat and free of defects. Apply mastic with notched trowel and set tiles. Tiles are flexible and conformable.

There is no paper to strip off with these tiles. Each section is held with flexible adhesive as shown clearly in this photo. Installer adjusts each sheet as necessary.

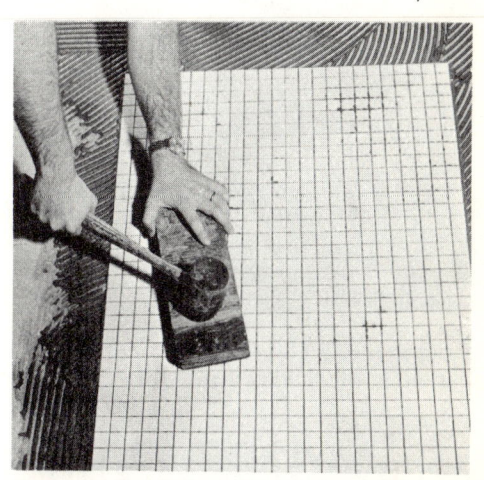

Preassembled tiles can also be used vertically on walls. Alignment is assured and the sheets will not sag. Each section is installed and embedded using rubbed-faced block.

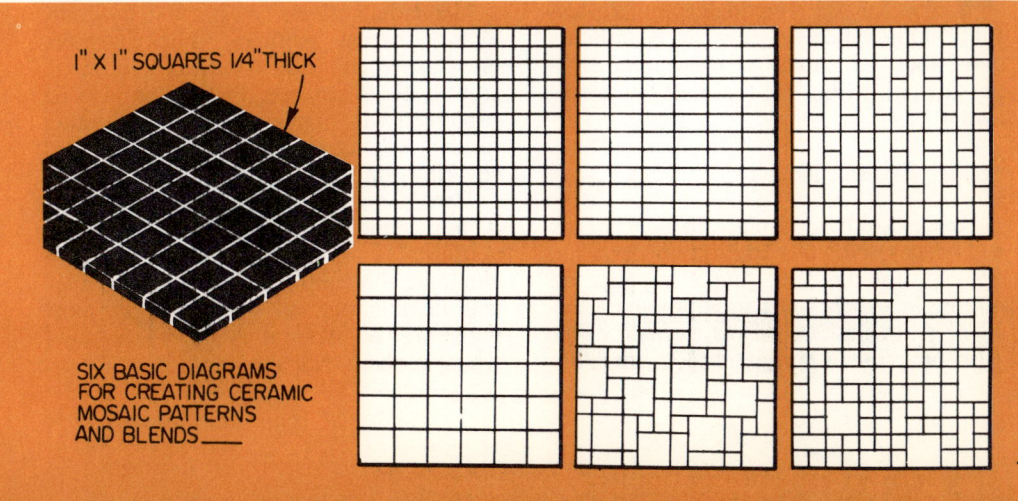

1" X 1" SQUARES 1/4" THICK

SIX BASIC DIAGRAMS FOR CREATING CERAMIC MOSAIC PATTERNS AND BLENDS

55

Conso Prod. Co.

Stock shades are easily turned into "custom specials" using a window shade kit. You cut the desired border and add your own trimming. Two rows of ball fringe were added to scallops.

WINDOW COVER-UPS

Spruce up that plain, old window

Windows offer an excellent opportunity for the remodeler to "do-his-stuff." Other than new draperies and curtains, there are many window treatments possible, all within the realm of the homeowner.

FIX UP THOSE SHADES

Shades are a good place to start. Many new decorative aids are on the market, designed for the do-it-yourselfer. Kits are offered in which you trim, applique, stencil or paint designs on plain shade cloth. Also offered are laminating kits for making your own shades with all-over patterns.

Handsome effects are possible by combining several methods. For example, press-on fringes can be added to a shade as well as its valance. Fringe can also be combined with laminations for interesting results. Appliques cut from fabrics or wall coverings offer infinite possibilities.

Decals can also be used for decorating. A note about add-ons: Try to limit the additions to the lower half of the shade to eliminate the possibility of wrinkling. Special flexible cement (available in most hardware or decorator stores) is used when working with shades.

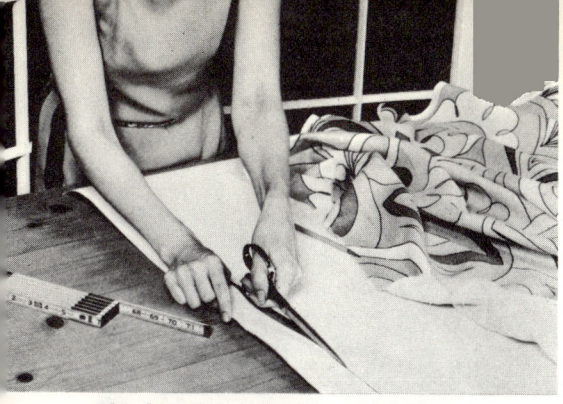

This kit allows the home decorator to make her own laminated window shades. Decorative fabrics are laminated to shade cloth. Shade cloth has a heat activated adhesive.

Photos Courtesy of Stauffer Chemical Co.

A 3" strip of shade cloth is measured and a line drawn. The decorative fabric is aligned on the pencil line. Overhang will be used later to heat seal cloth to the shade roller.

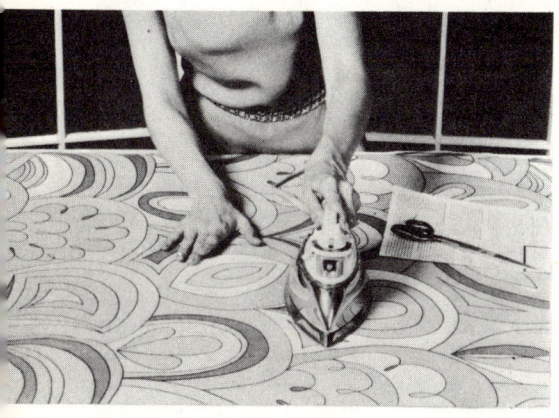

The fabric is laminated by use of a hot iron. Dry iron should be used and preheated to proper temperature for the fabric being used. The adhesive will make strong bond.

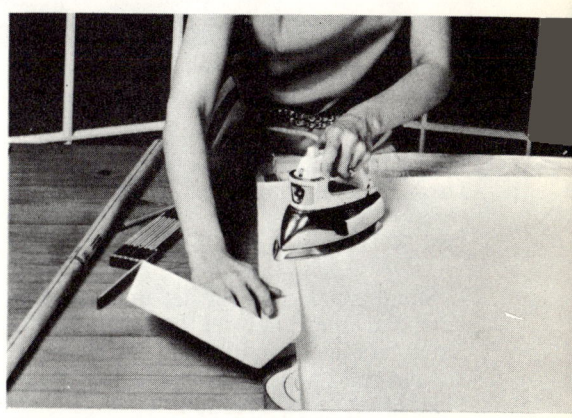

Slat hem for bottom of shade is made by folding over a 1½" strip at bottom of finished shade. A 2" strip of shade cloth is laminated to back of the shade to complete.

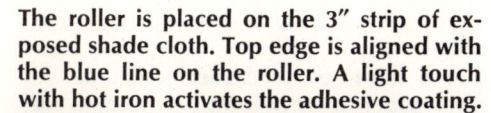

The roller is placed on the 3" strip of exposed shade cloth. Top edge is aligned with the blue line on the roller. A light touch with hot iron activates the adhesive coating.

PAINTING AND STENCILING SHADES

Painting on shades is easy and you don't have to be an artist. You can use stencils or work freehand. Use acrylic, vinyl-base latex, or textile paints. Just be sure to keep them thin, so the shade remains flexible.

Stenciling can be done with ready-made stencils purchased at art supply shops or you can cut your own. Use textile paints and apply with a stencil brush. Allow the paint to dry before removing the stencil. To make the stencil permanent, apply an

Simplest treatment for a window-wall is use of sheer, transparent draperies. This allows maximum light to enter and does not obstruct outside scenic view but allows for privacy.

iron at low heat for about five minutes. Use a press cloth between iron and shade.

ON SHUTTERS

Shutters are good for decorating a window and they can let you control the amount of light admitted into a room. Fabric and solid panel shutters are also available. Many stock sizes to fit most windows are offered.

ABOUT VALANCES AND CORNICES

Valances and cornices add greatly to the appearance of a room. You can use them to visually lower a ceiling or just to dress up a window. The cornice may top a single window or it may top all the windows against one wall, whichever gives the most pleasing effect. It is not only decorative, it is also functional as it conceals drapery and curtain rods and headings.

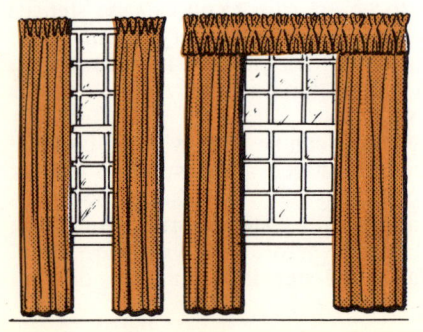

The cornice is usually made of plywood and resembles basically an upside-down window box. The cornice will protrude 4" to 12" from the wall, depending on the number of curtains and draperies it covers. It is attached to the walls and ceiling with angle brackets. The lower edge of the cornice can be straight or shaped in scallops or graceful curves. Trace the design you like on a piece of tracing paper, then transfer to lumber and cut with a sabre saw. The cornice may be painted or stained or covered with a fabric or wallpaper.

For a fabric covered cornice, simply lay your paper pattern down on the right side of fabric, allow 1½" (on all sides) for turning, cut out material. Staple the fabric to the wood, turning the 1½" allowance to the inner edge of the cornice. The bot-

BEFORE AFTER

Make tall, narrow window more eye-appealing. Here width is extended by rods mounted wider than window. Height is "lowered" by valance. Hang curtains and job is done.

Illinois Bronze Powder & Paint Co.

A lambrequin in the pattern and colors of your choice make a unique window treatment. All you need here are a design, stencil brush and acrylics. Buy or make stencils.

tom edge of the cornice may also be now trimmed with braid or fringe.

For a rich, elegant window dressing, a fabric covered cornice may also be upholstered. The fabric and plywood are cut to size as above, and a cotton padding and interlining must be inserted between. The cotton padding does not require the 1½" turning allowance, but the interlining and fabric covering do. Be sure to pull the fabric taut as you staple to prevent wrinkling. The bottom edge may be trimmed with decorative cording on the right side before attaching the fabric to the plywood.

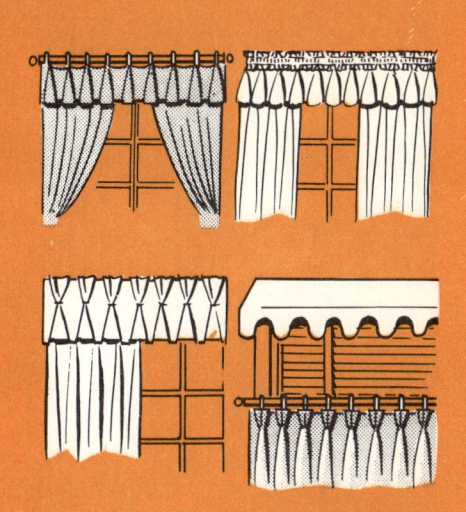

Velcro Corp.

Quick-and-Easy Fabric Valances

Four quick and easy styles of valances are shown. All are made of fabric. The first one is made like a regular pleated drape. Cafe rings are used to fasten to rod. The second one is perhaps the simplest, consisting of shirred ruffles on a cafe rod. The third is pleated on a curtain or traverse rod to give a tailored effect. The canopy style can be used on windows or over beds. Before attempting this one, make a paper pattern and carefully check fit to avoid cutting errors.

Make a paper pattern of the valance to check its appearance and proportions; transfer design to fabric, then cut out. Valance depth equals approximately ⅛th height of the drapery. Add 3" to length to allow for overlap at ends of window. From ¼" plywood (if length is over 40" use ¾"), make the valance board. Frame should just clear tops of fabric scallops. Fabric valance is attached to valance board with double-faced tape or you can use Velcro tape. *Velcro Corp.*

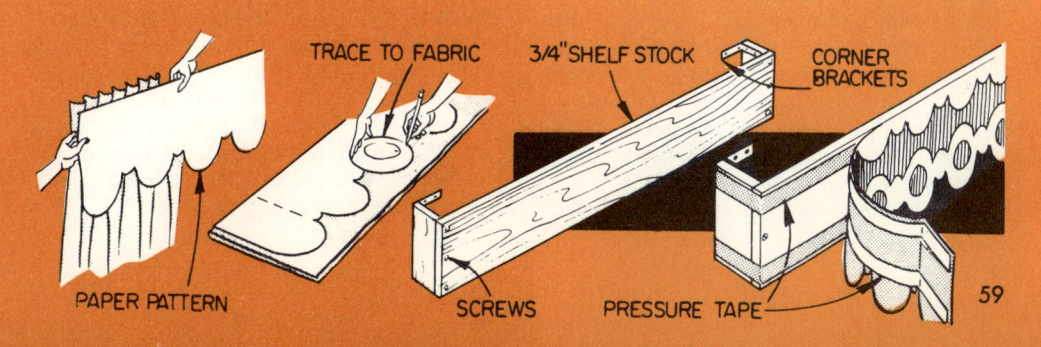

Ethan Allen

Solid shutters on this window are very effective. Contrasting design was done with moldings but they could also be painted on. Decorative tape is another versatile possibility.

COVERING UP BAD ARCHES

Ugly or poorly proportioned windows can be hidden by building an arched plywood framework and placing it in front of the windows and hanging full length drapes or curtains behind the arches. The arches create a more formal interior and look especially well in bedrooms and formal dining and living rooms. By placing such a framework against a plain solid wall, you can create the illusion of a window wall.

Filigree panels of either plywood or hardboard may also be used to make attractive cornices and arches. These panels are available at most lumber yards and you have a choice of many lovely patterns. For either the cornice or window arches, the filigree panels would be cut to size, then set into a wooden framework, and finished off with a suitable coat of paint. These panels allow more light to filter into a room and have a lovely airy effect.

Lambrequins, which are really simple cornices extended downward around the window frame to the floor level, are another alternative to your window problem. They too can be covered with wallpaper trims or fabric to emphasize your windows and add drama and beauty to your walls.

SIMPLE VALANCES YOU CAN MAKE

It takes the hands of an expert to create some of the elaborate swagged and draped valance treatments you'll see in this book and other leading decorating magazines.

But here, we show you five different styles that even the beginner dare tackle, for they are really quite simple to make.

There are two kinds: those hung on a curtain or cafe rod; and those which fasten to a wood support. In both cases, always cut a paper pattern first to determine the most pleasing depth in proportion to the total length of your draperies (usually $\frac{1}{6}$ to $\frac{1}{9}$). Pin the pattern to the tops of the draperies, then adjust until it looks pleasing. You're now ready to make it.

Plywood is generally used for valance face-piece if it is to be covered. If valance is to be painted, it is best to use pine. Trace outline onto board and cut with saber saw.

Box-like construction is used in making valance. Ends and top are joined first followed by face piece. Use glue and nails in construction. Countersink nails; cover with putty.

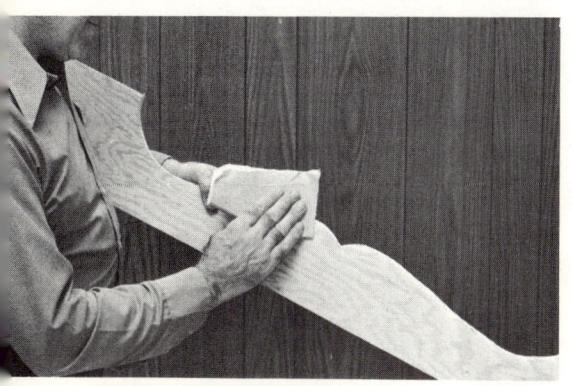

Good sanding is important. Do surface as well as the edges. Be especially careful of splinters when doing the edges. Height of valance is determined by type of window.

Spray-type adhesive simplifies covering of valance with fabric. Rough-cut the material to size then coat the backside with adhesive. Allow to become tacky, then apply slowly.

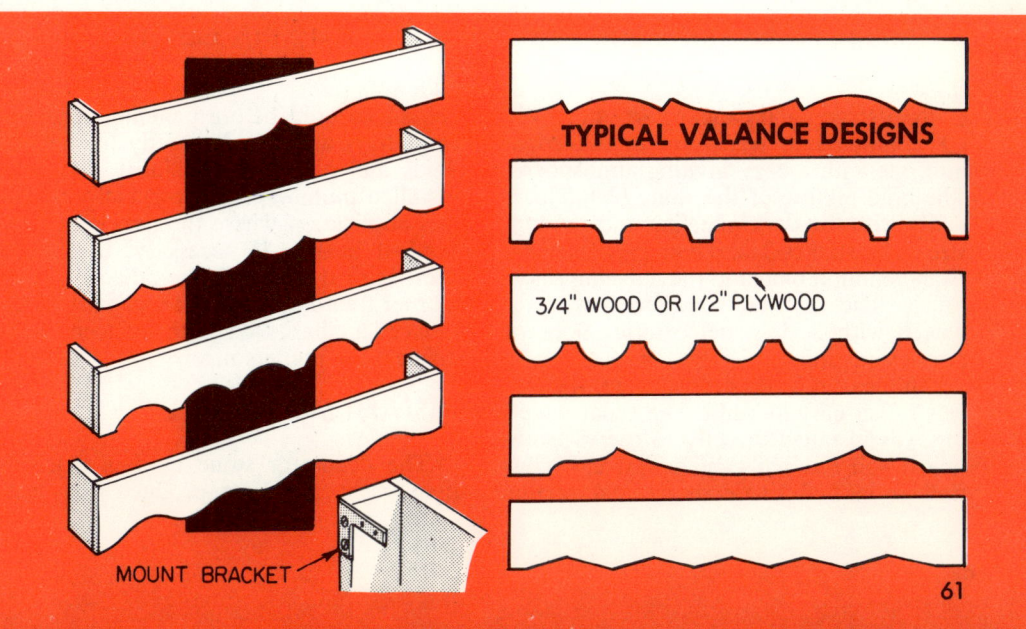

TYPICAL VALANCE DESIGNS

3/4" WOOD OR 1/2" PLYWOOD

MOUNT BRACKET

Den features fieldstone wall, rough beams and cedar shake shingles. Stone is synthetic but looks real. Beams are made by boxing ¾" pine or store-bought fake beams can be used.

A RUSTIC DEN

Paneling, fake stone and beams help simplify this easy-to-do job

Stone, shakes and paneling are effectively combined to transform a dull room into one with a cozy inviting atmosphere. The bold texture of the stone blends perfectly with the dark paneling and random size cedar shakes. Hand hewn beams made from common pine add the finishing rustic touch. The original solid door was replaced with a six-panel exterior door of ponderosa pine.

Although it looks complicated, the den was rather easy to build. The cedar paneling was installed directly to the gypsumboard wall with nails and adhesive. If your wall is in bad shape, horizontal furring should be used before paneling. The furring strips are nailed directly to the wall studs and plates. Panels must always be installed plumb. This is especially true in this application where the panels butt the vertical beams. If necessary, the panels are trimmed to match the adjacent walls. Corner treatments are not necessary as the red cedar shakes on both adjacent walls conceal the corners nicely.

INSTANT STONE WALL

The decorator stone used is a tough, lightweight polyester product that truly

Before photo reveals little of interest in room. Compare with photo of finished rustic den. Future plans call for wall to wall carpeting and also railing of turned spindles.

Roseburgs Mark V Mediterranean Cedar

Cedar paneling was installed directly over sound sheetrock wall. Adhesive was used and reinforced with nails, driven into studding. Color matching nails were used here.

Imitation stone by Dacor Mfg. Co. is applied with special adhesive mortar. Stones are random size and fitting is done beforehand to assure a good appearance and proper fit.

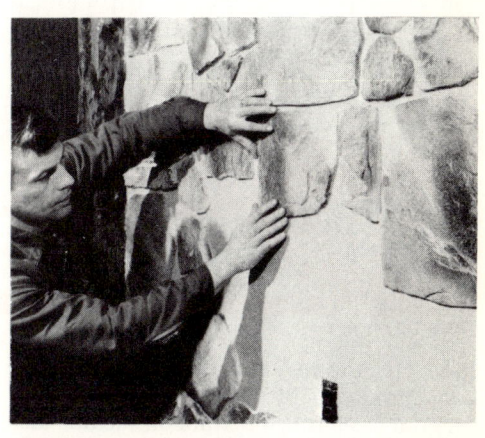

Stones are slid gently into place. The adhesive on wall between stones becomes the "mortar" joint. Adhesive is available in natural or black tone. Both give rich results.

Molding around door is fitted and temporarily installed. Remove for staining then replace permanently. Paneled door or ponderosa pine is also stained to match molding.

Cedar shakes are excellent for interior as well as exterior use. They are durable, economical, and need little maintenance. Installation starts near floor. Nail backboard.

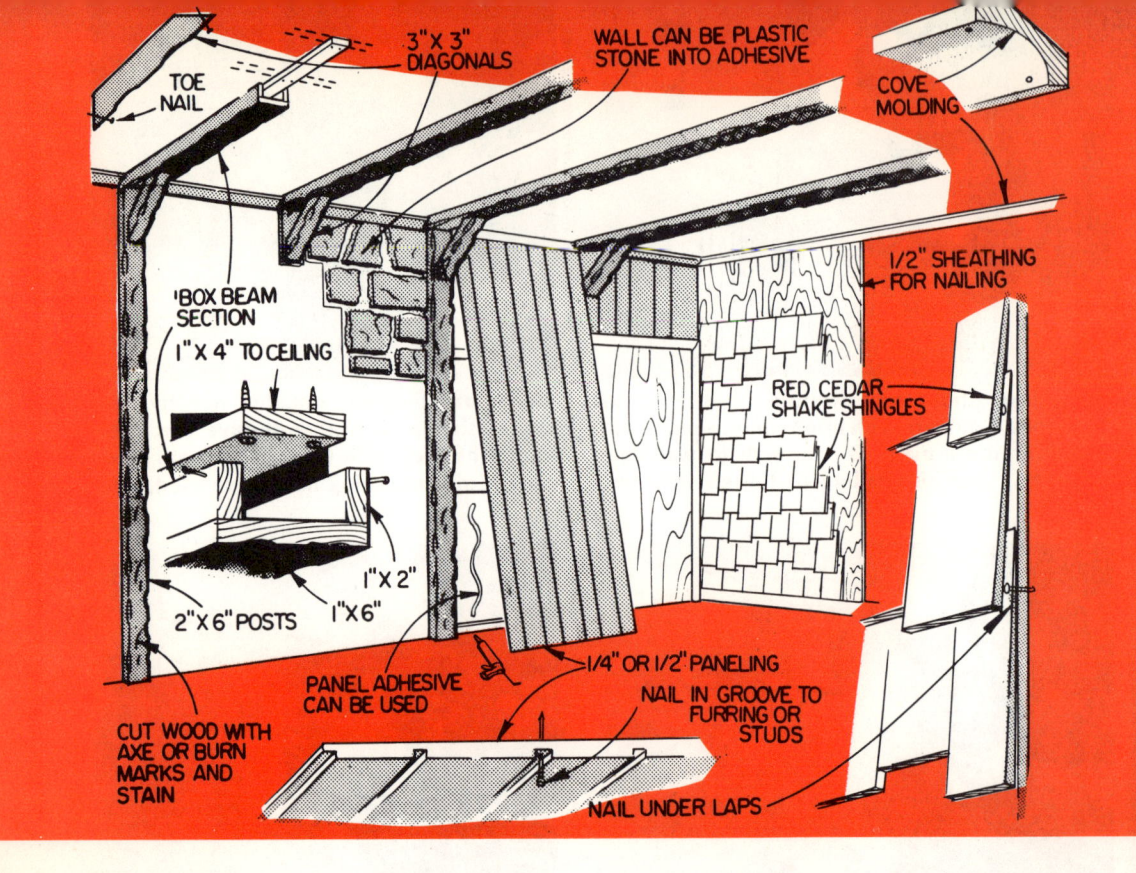

[Illustration labels: TOE NAIL; 3"X 3" DIAGONALS; WALL CAN BE PLASTIC STONE INTO ADHESIVE; COVE MOLDING; 1/2" SHEATHING FOR NAILING; BOX BEAM SECTION 1"X 4" TO CEILING; RED CEDAR SHAKE SHINGLES; 1"X 2"; 1"X 6"; 2"X 6" POSTS; PANEL ADHESIVE CAN BE USED; 1/4" OR 1/2" PANELING; NAIL IN GROOVE TO FURRING OR STUDS; NAIL UNDER LAPS; CUT WOOD WITH AXE OR BURN MARKS AND STAIN]

duplicates the real stuff. We used Oxford stone produced by Dacor Mfg. Co. The material has a rough texture on the outside but the back is smooth so that it can be applied to any flat surface easily.

A special adhesive mortar is spread thinly (about $\frac{1}{16}$") over the entire surface to be covered. This is the base coat which provides a rough surface to which the "stones" will adhere. After the base coat has dried, the stones are applied by buttering the backs as shown. The installation may start at the ceiling or floor and the work can be interrupted at any time. Stones are simply buttered and pressed into place. They should be placed at random to avoid the appearance of a repeat pattern.

CEDAR SHAKE WALL

The cedar shake wall is installed over $\frac{3}{8}$" plywood sheathing. This provides a nailing surface for the shakes. Undercourse shingles were used because of their knots which added to the desired rustic effect. The shakes must be installed from the floor up. A chalk line may be used to line up the rows or a temporary cleat can be installed.

The hand hewn beams across ceiling and wall are of boxlike construction. One-inch lumber is glued-up with butt joints in the shape of a "U." The fourth member is not attached. Instead, it is mounted to the wall or ceiling and the glued-up section is then mounted to it.

The lumber can be distressed in many ways. An axe or chisel may be used to remove the large chunks of wood. A gouge will make the smaller cuts and grooves. A large nail or ice-pick will make the worm holes.

The braces are cut from solid lumber and distressed in the same manner as the beams.

The base and crown mouldings as well as the beams are stained to match the paneling. The shakes and stones are left natural.

Perhaps an easier way to go, is to buy ready-to-install **fake beams.** Available at decorator shops and most lumberyards, they are lightweight and pre-finished. All you do is attach to walls or ceilings.

Armstrong Cork

This fully equipped kitchen and breakfast nook is done in cheerful yellow and white. No-wax flooring is ideal for kitchen, also resists scuffing and marking for easy care and durability.

KITCHEN CAPERS

Fast and easy kitchen improvements for the do-it-yourselfer

More remodeling takes place in the kitchen than any other room in the house. Major remodeling can be rather complicated, involving the installation or rerouting of plumbing and wiring and even sometimes the removal of a load-bearing wall. This may well be more than the average do-it-yourselfer can cope with.

If you are qualified and have sufficient knowledge and experience, go right ahead. Most appliance and utility companies have kitchen planning services which can help you design your "dream kitchen."

The suggestions on these pages are within the realm of the average homeowner and with patience and elbow grease you may well be on the way toward having a perfect kitchen.

EFFICIENT USE OF STORAGE SPACE

One often heard complaint from housewives is the lack of sufficient storage space.

Actually, available space is usually not being used efficiently. Special drawers are available which utilize unused or wasted corner space. Doors of cabinets can be used to advantage to hold cutting boards, flat pans and pot covers. Sliding partitions in the base of cabinets is another way to use every inch of space. See our section on storage regarding back-of-door shelves.

An island can be built to make use of kitchen floor space. The island can serve as a work and storage center. The top can be covered with laminated plastic or ceramic

Pass-through window in kitchen opens into den or dining room and saves many steps. Cutting through wall is a simple task, but check to insure that wall clears utilities.

This post running through kitchen countertop could not be removed so counter was built around it. Insert can be installed permanently with glue, removably with screws.

Plenty of storage in this kitchen cabinet. Lazy Susan and door shelves increase usable space. The door standards are mounted with screws. Shelves can be adjusted as desired.
Amerock

tiles or a thick maple top which will also serve as a cutting board. The island can be mounted on casters so it can be rolled about thus increasing its usefulness.

Maple tops can be purchased in various widths and lengths. Thickness ranges from 1½" upwards. If a laminated plastic top is desired, the top should be ¾" particle board or a good grade of plywood. Particle board is perfectly flat and ideally suited for laminates.

The accompanying sketch shows an easy way to build an island for your kitchen. It can be modified in size to suit your needs.

KITCHEN UPDATE

A simple way to update a kitchen is to brighten up your existing cabinets. You can spruce up a drab cabinet by replacing the hardware. Attractive pulls and knobs are available in many styles, materials and finishes.

Moldings and inserts can also be used to advantage. See our chapter on instant magic with moldings. You may want to try an adhesive-backed covering for dramatic effects. The advantage of using these

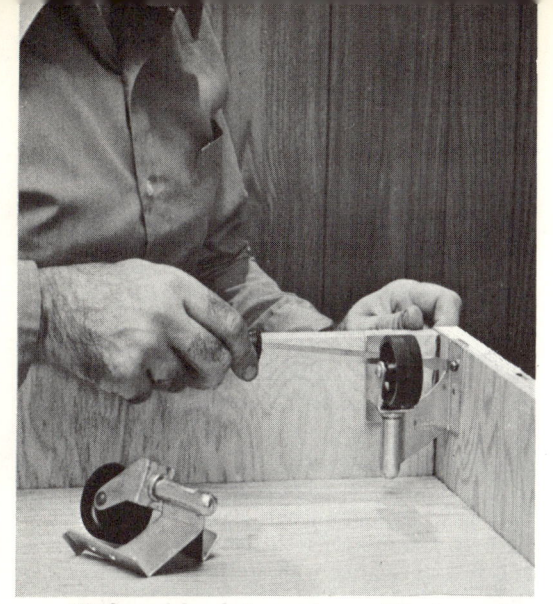

Kitchen island is made mobile by using bracket casters which mount at the corners behind the kick space. Wheels of swivel caster protrude 3/8" from the cabinet base.

To obtain thicker edge for countertop, strips of wood are added around perimeter. Plywood may be used if top is to be laminated, otherwise solid lumber with rabbet joints.

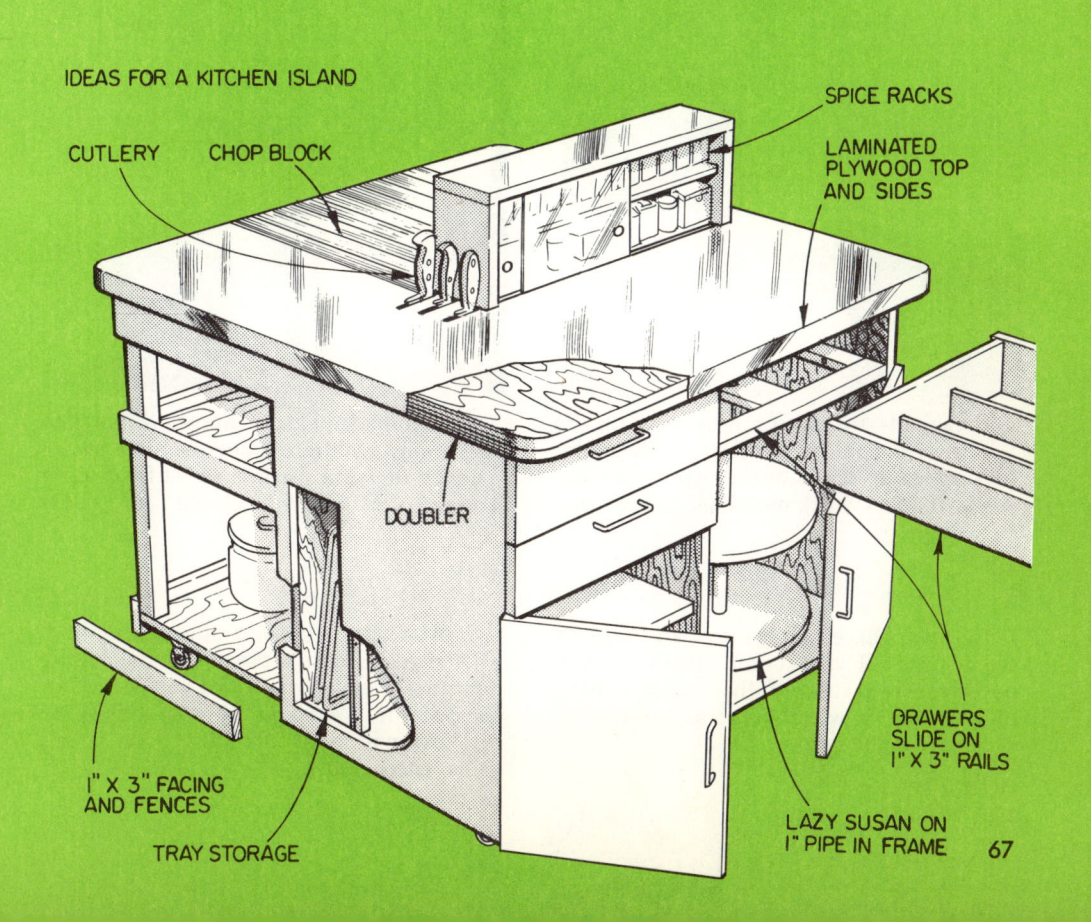

IDEAS FOR A KITCHEN ISLAND

- CUTLERY
- CHOP BLOCK
- SPICE RACKS
- LAMINATED PLYWOOD TOP AND SIDES
- DOUBLER
- 1" X 3" FACING AND FENCES
- TRAY STORAGE
- DRAWERS SLIDE ON 1" X 3" RAILS
- LAZY SUSAN ON 1" PIPE IN FRAME

67

Boos

Maple chopping block makes the job of food preparation easier. If you don't have room for a free standing unit, you can purchase an easy to install countertop. Sizes vary.

St. Charles of N.Y. City, Inc.

This well planned kitchen leaves little to be desired. Countertops are laminated plastic and sink and range wall are tough stainless steel, resulting in a very easy maintenance.

Old cabinets are given a new lease on life with new decorative hardware. Bold moldings added to doors and drawers can also work wonders. Stock moldings can be used.

Dutch doors are ideal in homes where there are young children. Upper section can be opened in warm weather to let fresh air in. Lower part remains closed for safety.

is that you can easily remove and replace the material if you should tire of it. The coverings look best if the cabinets have molded panels which serve as a frame to contain the material.

Most kitchens have insufficient lighting. This can be easily remedied by adding luminous panels or ceilings in your kitchen. See the special sections in this book for information on updating your floors, walls, and ceilings.

Armstrong Cork

The traditional influence in this room is unmistakable, especially with the colonial style tile ceiling and fake-candle chandelier. Tiles cover old ceilings easily for a smashing effect.

CLOSE-UP ON CEILINGS

Tile it, add fake beams, lower it—the possibilities are many

Overhead ceilings used to be drab and purely functional. They are still functional but no longer drab. Ceilings, like the walls in your house, can be painted, papered, paneled, beamed, tiled, suspended and even illuminated.

When old ceilings show signs of age and begin to crack, show water stains, and nails begin to pop, then it's time to repair or renew them. You'll find it is easier to recover the existing ceiling with tiles than to replaster and repaint. Before going ahead with any recovering job, be sure to remedy the cause of those water stains.

TIPS ON TILES

You will find a wide selection of ceiling tiles on the market today. You must choose from acoustical or non-acoustical, vinyl-surfaced (scrubbable), embossed, two-tone, and smooth surfaced in many decorator styles. The tiles are usually 12" square and installation is easy enough for children to tackle.

Daub ceiling cement on each corner of the tile and also in the center, then press firmly into position on the ceiling. The tiles have tongue-and-groove joints which in-

69

All the supplies and tools needed to install an acoustical tile ceiling are shown. Although tiles will be installed on dry wall ceiling, no adhesive is used, only staples.

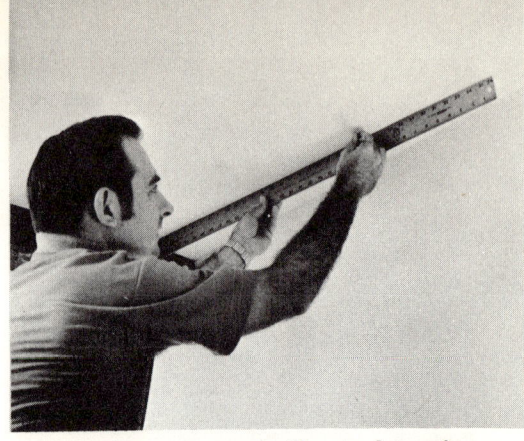

First step is to measure ceiling to determine centerline. Few ceilings are perfectly sized for 12" x 12" or 2' x 4' panels. First row should start at centerline so edges are even.

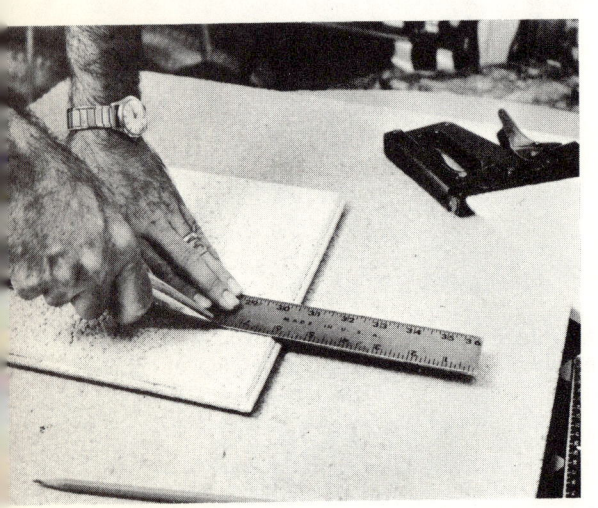

A sharp knife, and metal straight edge are needed to properly cut ceiling tile. This tile will butt up against a ceiling beam so it is cut at 45° angle to make a clean butt joint.

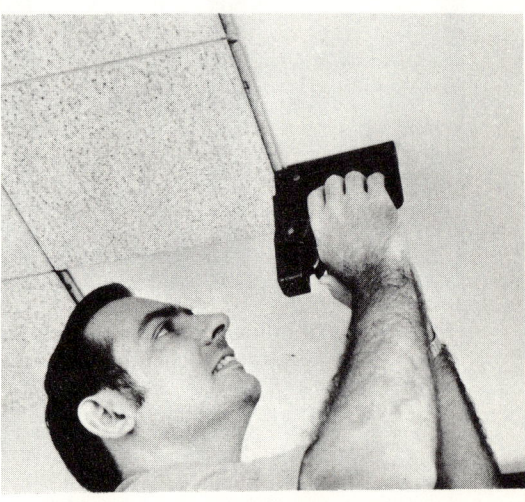

Simple way to install ceiling tiles on gypsum dry wall is using "piggy-back" staples as shown. One staple is driven in first and another driven directly over it to anchor.

terlock making for straight installation. A couple of staples in exposed flanges will hold the tile in place while the adhesive sets. That's it. Job's done!

PLANK CEILINGS

Ceiling tiles are also available in plank form, each 4 ft. long and in varying widths. They also can be stapled to furring strips or cemented to an existing ceiling. They are available in wood-grain or etched surface and have the advantage of fast installation due to their size.

FAKE BEAMS

Beamed ceilings are a favorite for family rooms, but they are also being used in kitchens and bedrooms. Synthetic beams

70

Western Wood Prod. Assn.
Here's a new twist for a ceiling. Wall of 1" x 8" western red cedar was continued up and across ceiling. Accurate measurements and careful cutting eliminate the need for moldings.

made of lightweight styrofoam are easily installed on ceilings as well as walls. The beams are so realistic that it is hard to tell a real one from a "fake." The beams can be fastened with nails, screws or adhesive, and can be cut to size with ordinary tools.

LOWERING THE CEILING

Suspended ceilings are not as difficult to install as they may seem, and they have an added advantage that the ceiling may be illuminated to your liking at the same time. Suspended grid units which support the tiles are wired to the ceiling. Decorator tiles may be used or in the case of a luminous ceiling, translucent plastic panels may be installed instead.

Dramatic decorative effects can be obtained by using brilliantly colored printed fabrics and wallcoverings on your ceiling. Be sure they don't clash with the decor.

71

Cozy family room features paneled wall and suspended acoustical ceiling. One section of ceiling is illuminated, yielding soft even light. The 24" x 48" panels go up very fast.

Armstrong photos

First step in installation is to nail molding to wall at desired ceiling height. This will support the panels at perimeter of room. Use care not to strike the molding edge.

Temporary string lines help locate hanger wires. String is placed at predetermined ceiling height. Hanger wires are attached to joists at 4-foot intervals. Twist several times.

Main runners of metal framework are suspended by means of the hanger wires. Twisting wires allows fine adjustment of runner. Note how block is used to span.

Cross tees are snapped into place between main runners. Tees are placed 2 ft. apart at 4 ft. intervals and they should engage slots fully and lock into place. Bend to fit.

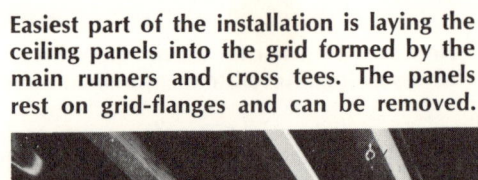

Easiest part of the installation is laying the ceiling panels into the grid formed by the main runners and cross tees. The panels rest on grid-flanges and can be removed.

ATTICS AND BASEMENTS
Renovate them to create new storage space plus extra living space

Some families will go out looking for a new home instead of utilizing wasted space in their present home. Attics and basements especially are ideal for expanding storage areas, recreational facilities, and extra living and bedroom quarters.

The walls, floor, and ceiling are already there. You may wish to add electrical wiring and plumbing, for which you may need professional help, but the cost is small compared to the price of another home in today's market.

NOTES ON BASEMENTS

Basements, besides serving their function of storing a furnace or hot water heater, can be remodeled into one or more usable rooms. See previous chapters in this book on coverings available for floors, walls, ceilings. These can be easily done by the homeowner himself at his leisure and when his finances permit.

This basement left much to be desired. Clutter and "dead end" stairway were two problems. Solution was to conceal heater and steer traffic into a recreation room.

73

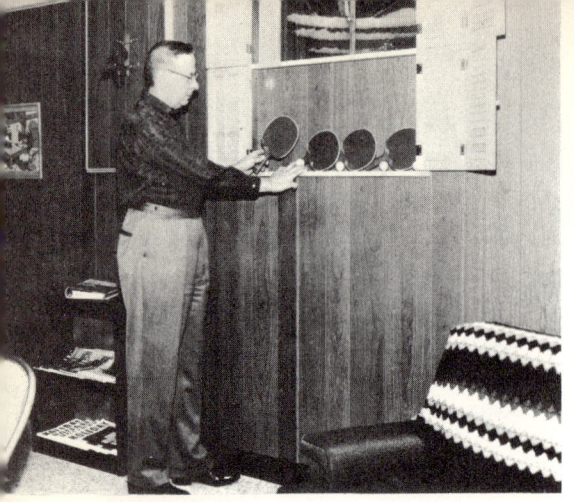

Masonite photos

A double set of louvered doors serves two purposes here. Upper set covers the window and lower closes to hide Ping-pong balls and paddles. Perforated backboard is useful.

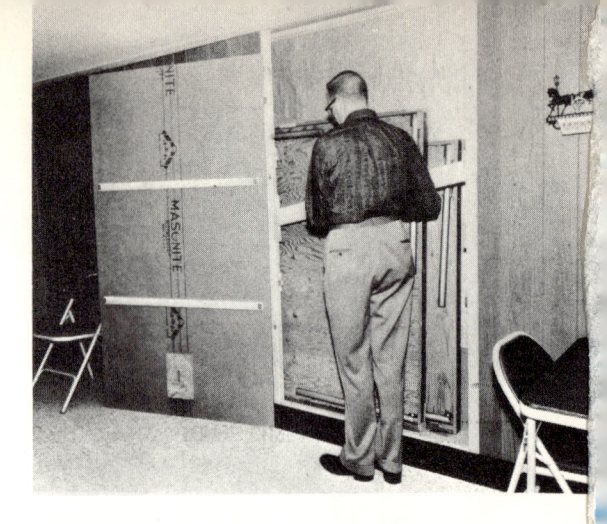

This shallow hide-away holds folded regulation size Ping-pong table. The hardboard panels are lift-outs, giving complete access to the floor-to-ceiling space that is behind.

Operating on the principle of sliding doors, the panels are first lifted up, then down and out by means of a finger latch. Slots in bottom and top plates make for easy operation.

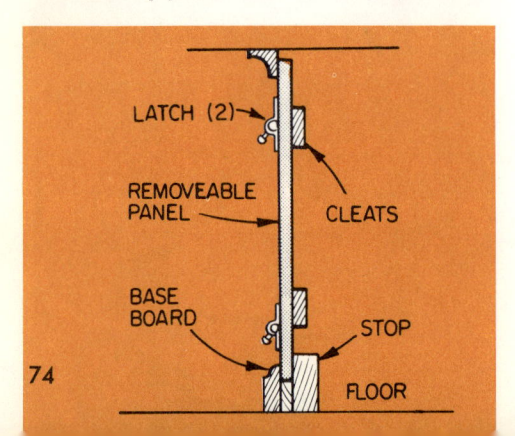

When designing the basement, *be sure to include ample storage facilities*. No matter how large the home, there never seems to be enough of this precious commodity. Make use of the space under the stairs. This area can be left open with suitable shelving, or covered with sliding or hinged doors. Another possibility is to make a series of drawers.

Pipes, meters, and the like can be usually concealed by boxing or partitioning. Be sure to *leave all valves and cleanouts accessible*.

If dampness is a problem, this should be corrected before any work is begun. Waterproofing compounds are available. In addition, vapor barriers are used to further check dampness. Dehumidifiers are helpful but they should be used in addition to the waterproofing, not instead of.

There are excellent floorings available for basements. Choose one suitable for your particular conditions. Your flooring dealer can give you good advice here.

Don't neglect good lighting for your basement. Without it, all other remodeling is practically wasted. No one wants to live in a dark dungeon, even if it does have very fine walls and floors.

A once barren attic has become an attractive room suitable for study, hobby pursuits, lounging and sleeping. Rough-textured hardboard siding runs from kneewall across the ceiling.

THE BASEMENT TRANSFORMED

Whether your basement is large or small, storage hide-aways are a good idea. You can eliminate clutter and utilize every bit of floor space.

A Ping-pong table is an excellent candidate for hide-away storage. When not being used, the table can be a nuisance, occupying valuable floor space. Since most tables fold for storage, consider a shallow storage area when finishing your basement.

In addition to storage behind walls, you can also find a hiding place at the ceiling joists. Pipes, rods, moldings, clamps and lumber, are just a few of the items that will fit nicely between joists. Simply nail or screw a few cleats across the joists to support the materials. This idea works equally well on open or suspended ceilings.

The hide-away principle can also be used to conceal plumbing valves, circuit breakers, and gas and electric meters. The photos illustrate a removable panel but a sliding or hinged door design can also be used. Sliding door tracks are available for all thicknesses of hardboard and plywood.

Instead of paneling, you may want to use louvered doors. These are fine for breaking up the monotony of a large expanse of paneling. They need not open into a room or closet. They have been used quite effectively on a wall with the area behind only as deep as the studding. A series of shelves from floor to ceiling only 3½" deep can be most useful.

NOTES ON ATTICS

Attics are another excellent source of extra room in the home. They can be converted into playrooms, sewing rooms, office or even a den. The ceiling of course will pose a problem. The walking area of an attic is limited because of the slanting roof but you can utilize the available space by careful planning. The low areas can be used for beds, desks, built-ins, etc.

If a dormer is in the plans, it's best to have a professional do the structural work. You can still do the interior finishing and save considerably on labor costs.

The drawing shows a typical attic framed and ready for walls. Use this as a guide in planning yours.

75

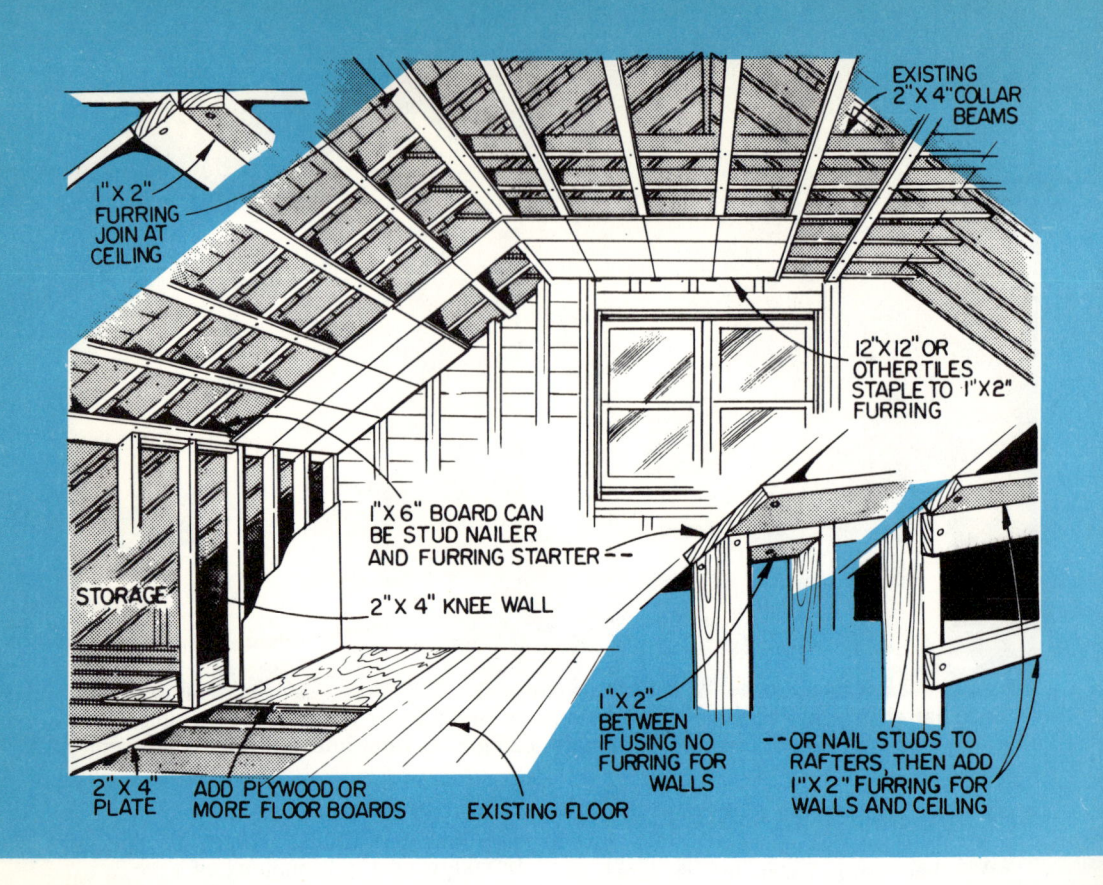

Diagram labels:
- 1" X 2" FURRING JOIN AT CEILING
- EXISTING 2" X 4" COLLAR BEAMS
- 12" X 12" OR OTHER TILES STAPLE TO 1" X 2" FURRING
- 1" X 6" BOARD CAN BE STUD NAILER AND FURRING STARTER
- 2" X 4" KNEE WALL
- STORAGE
- 2" X 4" PLATE
- ADD PLYWOOD OR MORE FLOOR BOARDS
- EXISTING FLOOR
- 1" X 2" BETWEEN IF USING NO FURRING FOR WALLS
- OR NAIL STUDS TO RAFTERS, THEN ADD 1" X 2" FURRING FOR WALLS AND CEILING

The attic is well on its way to becoming a modern livable room. Heating unit and insulation have already been installed. Next step is paneling. Behind kneewall is storage.

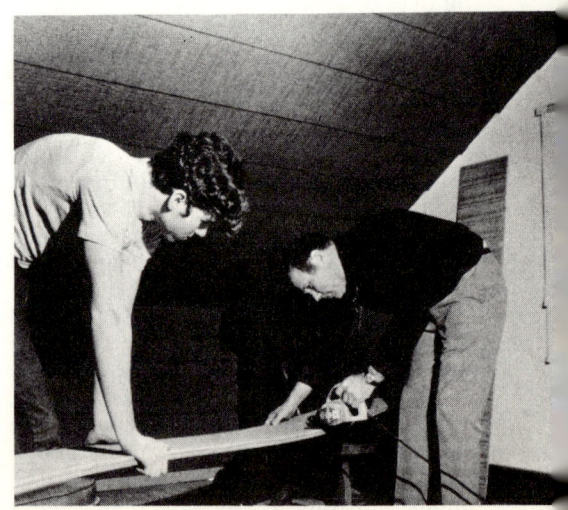

The hardboard siding used here comes in 16-foot lengths, and goes up fast. The outdoor siding is very popular, can be easily cut with those ordinary woodworking tools.

The Masonite Ruf-X siding used for lining the rafters is finished as desired. Here it is being stained. The material can also be painted or left natural, the choice is yours.

Masonite photos

The lapped siding strips which were pre-stained were coated with a clear dull varnish. Grooved nails are used to install them to rafters. One edge of siding is grooved.

This nautical attic room was finished off with Marlite paneling. The pegboard dividers separate the room into compartments so each child has his or her own area to use.

Marlite

Make your attic room cozy, comfortable and casual with a luxurious shag rug. Decorate the walls with adjustable shelves and adhesive-backed vinyl wallcovering and enjoy.

Armstrong

Colorful laminated boxes can be used as individual coffee tables or brought together to make one large table. Excellent when you need more table space. Cubes are very easy to make.

BEAUTY IN BOXES

Transform a simple box or cube into a modular piece of furniture

You can do so much with boxes about the home. Stacked, they make excellent storage shelves. Used individually, they can serve as end tables, coffee tables, night tables, etc. Put a door on a box and it becomes a cabinet.

Start with a simple box made of low-cost lumber and cover it with one of the following: paint, plastic laminate, self-adhesive plastic, ceramic tiles, parquet squares, fabric, vinyl, and even campaign chest hardware. Here are instructions for building a basic box or cube. The decorating material is left to you for there are so many available.

Unless the box is to be painted or stained, ordinary butt joints may be used in the construction. If the joints will show, they should be rabbeted or mitered. The rabbeted joint is far easier to make than the mitered and it is highly recommended. Boxes to be covered can be made with

Parts to be laminated must be clean and free of dust. Apply contact cement to both laminate and work and allow to set. Recoat dull spots; join when adhesive isn't sticky.

Laminate is carefully positioned on work and pressed into place. Positioning must be accurate as laminate cannot be repositioned once it has made contact with work surface.

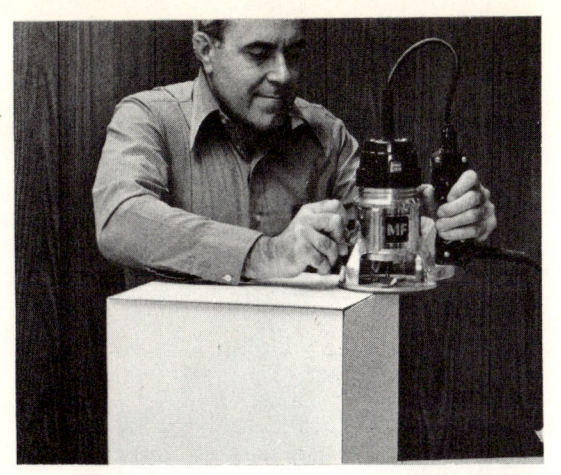

Slight overhang at edges is quickly trimmed with router. Special cutters will bevel the edges slightly. Lacking a router, a file can be used to do the trimming but it takes longer.

Finished box is given professional look with brass hardware. Before mounting hardware, locate and drill pilot holes for the escutcheons as laminate is brittle and it may crack.

butt-joints. No matter what type joint, be sure glue is used in addition to nails or screws. Sand all rough edges and sink all nail heads.

Most lumber yards will cut lumber to size, so if you figure your dimensions beforehand you can have your dealer do most of the work for you.

A good choice for boxes is plywood in either ½" or ¾" thickness. If your plans call for a wood-grained box, use ½" plywood and cover with prefinished panel-

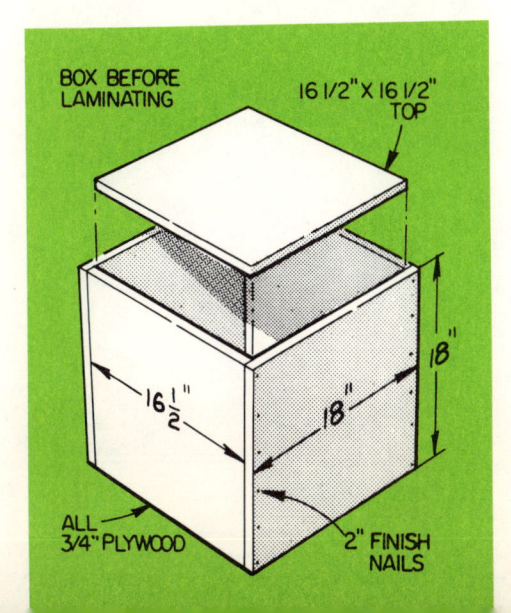

BOX BEFORE LAMINATING
16 1/2" X 16 1/2" TOP
16 1/2"
18"
18"
ALL 3/4" PLYWOOD
2" FINISH NAILS

Boxes can serve many purposes. This one complete with campaign chest hardware and hard surfaced laminate makes a neat and useful table. It has a dummy drawer front.

HOW TO INSTALL LAMINATE TO ANY SURFACE

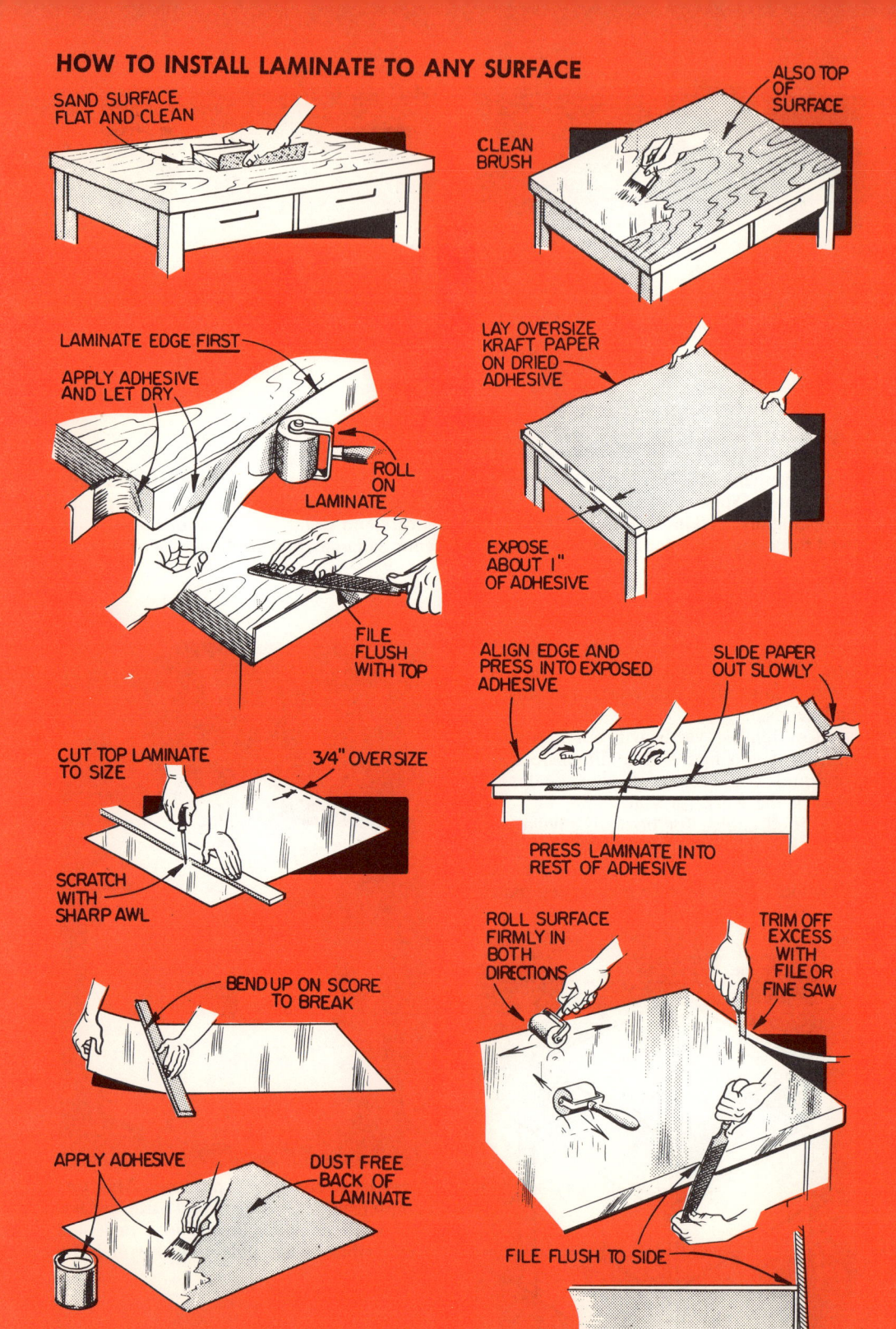

- SAND SURFACE FLAT AND CLEAN
- ALSO TOP OF SURFACE
- CLEAN BRUSH
- LAMINATE EDGE FIRST
- APPLY ADHESIVE AND LET DRY
- ROLL ON LAMINATE
- LAY OVERSIZE KRAFT PAPER ON DRIED ADHESIVE
- EXPOSE ABOUT 1" OF ADHESIVE
- FILE FLUSH WITH TOP
- ALIGN EDGE AND PRESS INTO EXPOSED ADHESIVE
- SLIDE PAPER OUT SLOWLY
- CUT TOP LAMINATE TO SIZE
- 3/4" OVERSIZE
- SCRATCH WITH SHARP AWL
- PRESS LAMINATE INTO REST OF ADHESIVE
- BEND UP ON SCORE TO BREAK
- ROLL SURFACE FIRMLY IN BOTH DIRECTIONS
- TRIM OFF EXCESS WITH FILE OR FINE SAW
- APPLY ADHESIVE
- DUST FREE BACK OF LAMINATE
- FILE FLUSH TO SIDE
- AVOID SCRAPING SIDE

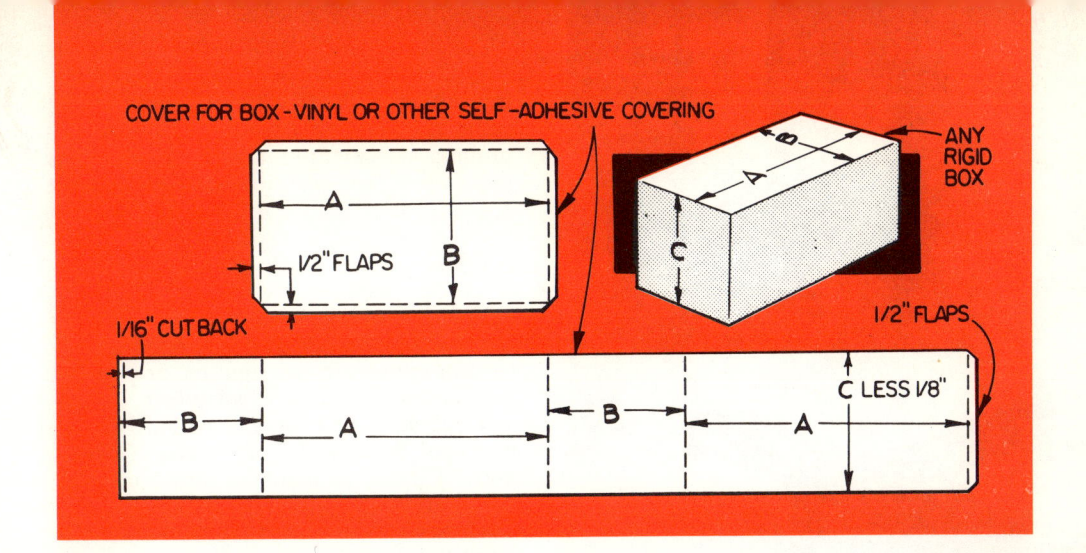

COVER FOR BOX - VINYL OR OTHER SELF-ADHESIVE COVERING

- 1/2" FLAPS
- ANY RIGID BOX
- 1/16" CUT BACK
- 1/2" FLAPS
- C LESS 1/8"

Box to be covered with shag carpet is made of ¾" plywood. Outside finished size should be 17½" in height, width and depth. Bottom panel is not needed. Nail and glue.

Using a sharp knife, trim the carpet on all four edges, leaving a 45-degree bevel all around. A pencil line ¼" in from the edge is used as a guide for cutting the miters.

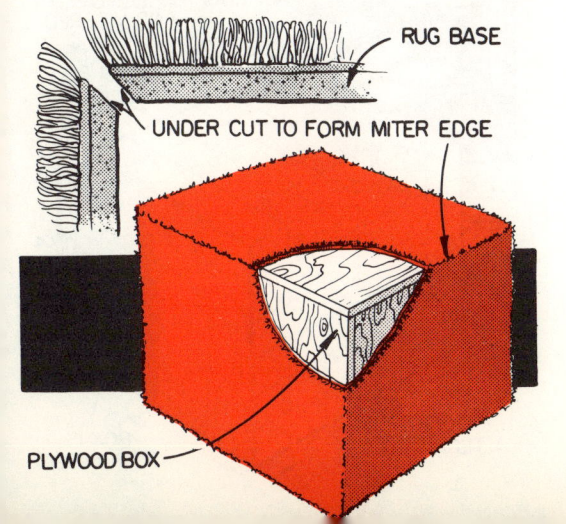

RUG BASE
UNDER CUT TO FORM MITER EDGE
PLYWOOD BOX

The mitered corners of this carpet should fit perfectly. While this carpet has a self-adhesive feature, it is not sticky enough for vertical application so use glue or tape.

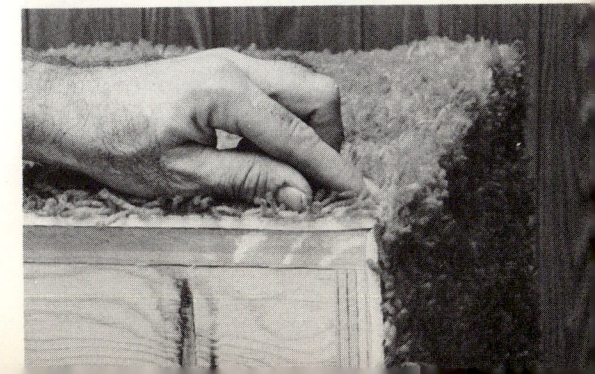

This elegant end table was made of plywood and covered with parquet squares. You can use left-over squares from a flooring job or make from paneling scraps.

Squares for decorating box are cut from scrap paneling. Rip length to proper width then cut off sections to form squares. Check size carefully as a slight error will be seen.

ing, either with or without grooves. The same box can be covered with a wood-grained self-adhesive plastic. It won't be real wood, but one would have to look really close to tell the difference.

NOVEL USES FOR BOXES

If you have parquet squares left over from a flooring job, you can build a truly elegant cube with the squares, or you can use them to cover an existing box.

Decorative campaign chest hardware is excellent for dressing up a box. Corners and "T"s are available in brass together with matching pulls.

Here's another novel use for boxes. Cut hand holes at the top near the open end, add casters to the bottom, and paint brightly. A few made this way are ideal for use as rolling toy boxes for children.

Try your hand at making these boxes. Once you discover how easy they are to build, you'll think of many new original uses and decorating ideas. You'll find it's easy on the budget too.

FINAL NOTES ON BOXES

Painted or tiled boxes are also popular. You can add partitions, shelves or doors, using them for any number of chores. Ceramic tile covered boxes are ideal for use as tables, or else, turn them upside down for a fancy durable planter. Extend the sides, making the box about 20" tall and you will wind up with a beautiful umbrella stand.

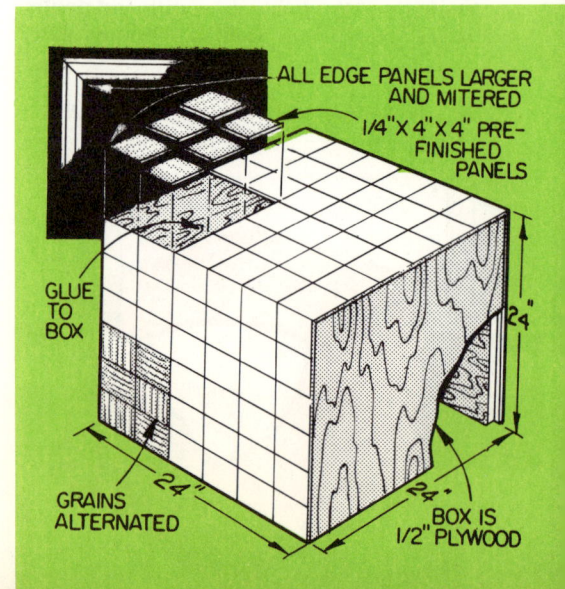

This handsome chest was made with plywood and covered with scrap squares of paneling. The squares are simply cut to size on the table saw and glued onto box. Brass hardware adds grand finale.

Tiles are held with mastic. Build the box so the tiles will not require cutting. This is not always possible, of course. If you have a few pieces to cut, mark the cutting line then have the local tile shop cut them out for you. If you have many to cut, you can rent a tile cutter for a couple of dollars.

Open joints should be grouted. If you like, you can purchase special colors to mix with the grout so the grout will match or complement the tile.

For painted boxes, your best bet is to use a board called MDO. These initials stand for medium density overly. This is a plywood board which has a special surface coating especially suited for painting. This surface is smooth, does not show the grain of the wood and is easily painted. It is entirely waterproof and can be used indoors or out.

WOOD PARQUET CHEST

This chest is not as difficult to make as it seems. The basic box is made of ½" plywood assembled with plain butt joints. Make the box as a single unit then cut it

Use white glue to cement squares because it sets fast and dries clear without staining. Apply glue to backs of squares in zigzag then brush out. Air dry slightly; assemble.

Parquet effect is achieved by alternating grain direction of each square. To obtain good contact between mating surfaces, slide the glued blocks into their position.

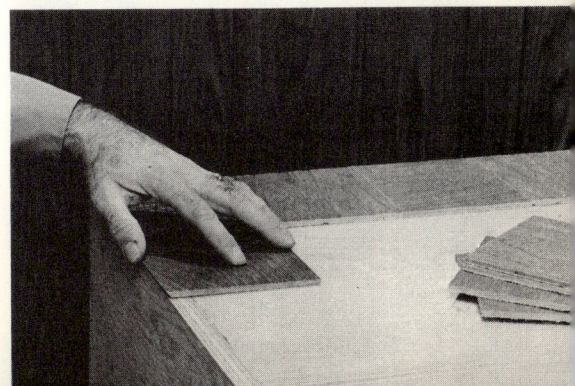

1/4" PANELING ON 1/2" PLYWOOD

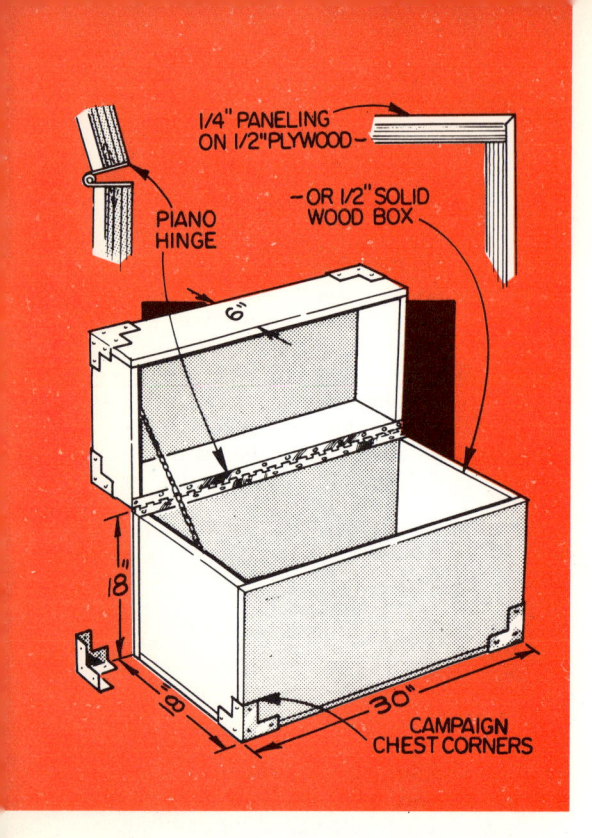

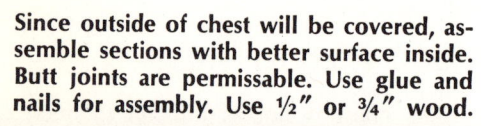

PIANO HINGE

— OR 1/2" SOLID WOOD BOX

6"

18"

18"

30"

CAMPAIGN CHEST CORNERS

A flat surface is important when laminating. After assembly and when glue has set, sink all nail heads then sand edges. A belt sander does the job best, or use a plane.

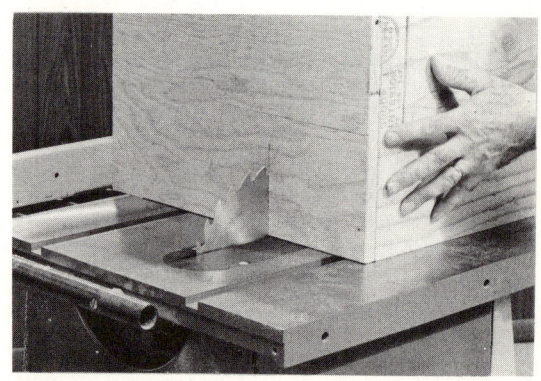

Since outside of chest will be covered, assemble sections with better surface inside. Butt joints are permissable. Use glue and nails for assembly. Use ½" or ¾" wood.

Base and lid are made as a single unit then cut apart on the table saw. Blade should be only ⅛" higher than thickness of wood. (In photo blade was raised higher for clarity.)

When covering the chest, cut end pieces longer to allow for the miter. A rabbet joint may also be used here. Apply glue to both surfaces of the miter and tape until set.

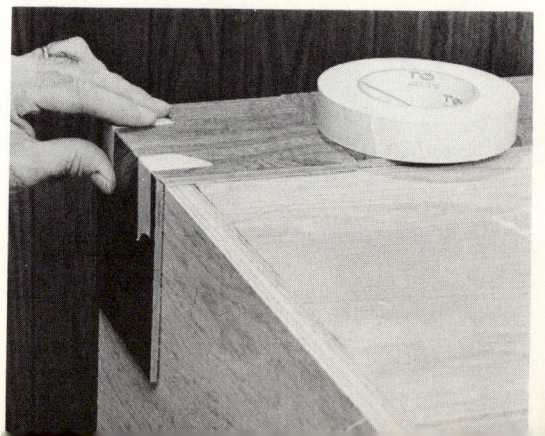

84

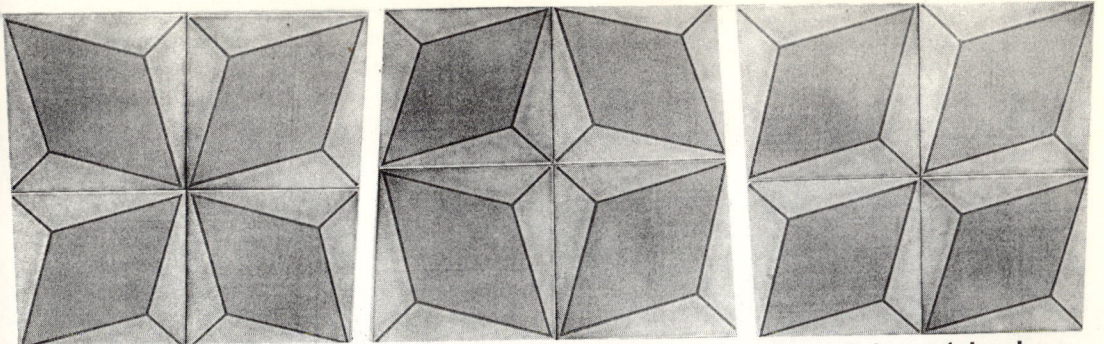

Patterned ceramic tiles may be used to create interesting designs. All three of the above designs were made by rearranging the same four 8" pieces of glazed tile. Try other designs.

apart on the table saw to form the lid. This will assure perfect alignment between the two sections.

The base and lid are covered with squares cut from ¼" paneling. Avoid using the grooves, if your paneling has any. The ends of the basic box are made with butt joints, but the laminated pieces should be mitered.

The best way to fasten the squares is with white glue. Apply thinned glue to both the work and the squares. Allow to air dry about a minute then slide into place. *Do not coat the whole box* with glue, *instead coat a section at a time.* Be sure to glue edges of squares too.

If the paneling you used is prefinished, simply paint the inside flat black then add hardware to complete the project. Unfin-

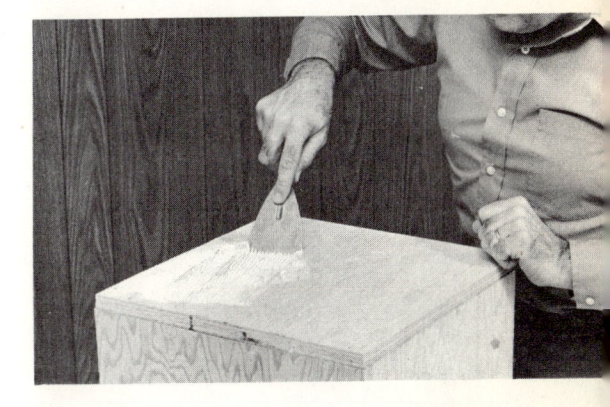

To tile a box, sand and dust the surface, then apply a coat of ceramic adhesive using a notched trowel. Work one surface at a time, and allow adhesive to become very tacky.

Tiles are set in mastic with edges of top overhanging the side. Adhesive is slow-drying so position the tiles until they are perfectly aligned. Large or small tiles available.

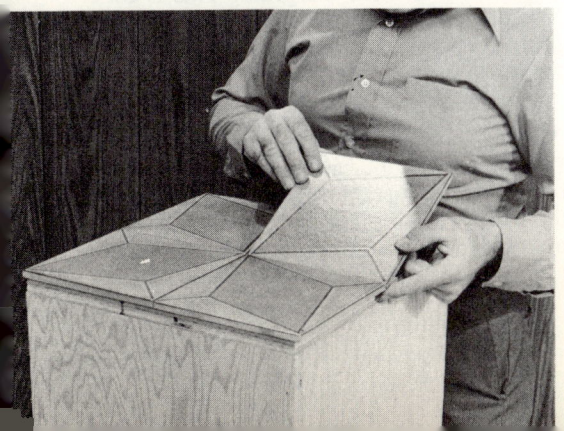

Before installing the vertical tiles, check fit carefully. The overhang and butt should align perfectly. If necessary, top tiles can be shifted before glue has had chance to set.

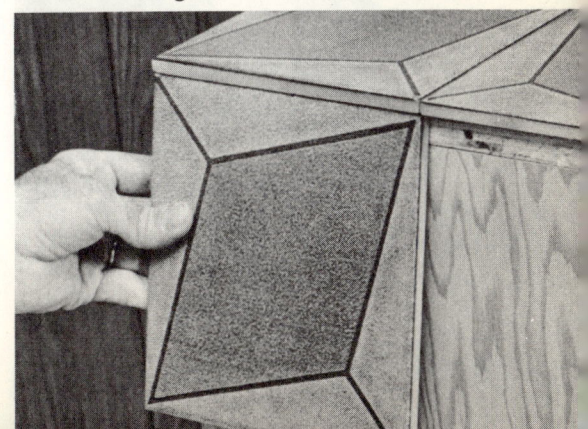

Cube with a door makes an excellent storage compartment. Several of these may be placed side by side or stacked. Doors may be painted in contrasting bright colors.

To make a toy box, build a 14" cube of ½" plywood using butt joints. Cut a hand hole at each end near the top. Sand all edges and finish with non-lead paint. Let dry overnight.

ished panels should be either stained or left clear followed by several coats of varnish or lacquer.

If the wood is an open grain type, it may be necessary to seal the pores before the finish coat is applied. Wood such as walnut or mahogany are good examples of open grained woods. A paste wood filler thinned to the consistency of heavy cream is brushed on with the grain. This is followed by rubbing the wood across the grain to remove excess filler. Follow with finish of your choice.

Two Plexiglas cubes are cleverly used here to form an etagere. The lower 16" cube protects the sculpture and the smaller 12" one on top serves as a terrarium. Material is easy to use and readily available at many stores.

Accessories, like the topping on a cake, can add zest to a drab wall or room. The recessed wall mural is bathed in soft light from a hidden fluorescent fixture. Clock and ship accent it.

WALL ACCESSORIES

Add color, beauty and interest to walls with distinctive trims

Mirrors are excellent accessories, adding dimension and depth to a wall. This one has a fancy carved frame and was purchased but the skilled homeowner can frame his own.

Beautiful accessories dress up walls just as curtains complement windows. They can be functional or decorative or combinations of both. They are important, also, since they reflect the homeowners personal taste and help make the house a home.

The most commonly used accessories are mirrors and pictures. These should be used sparingly and not overdone. Groups of pictures should avoid monotony by artistic arrangement and careful framing.

The frames should not detract from the subject matter of the pictures, but they should contrast with the wall background. Try making your own frames with moldings bought from the lumberyards.

Three dimensional accessories are very important in dressing up a wall. These include shelves, sconces, clocks, plaques, curio cabinets, etc.

87

Lumber yards sell numerous accessories which can be used as is or transformed into useful objects. Wagon wheels can be made into tables by adding legs and glass top.

Wood letters and numerals can be effectively used indoors and out for ornamental purposes. Dens and children's rooms are likely places for them. Try making a mobile.

Heavy wood shelves are in large demand these days. You can buy or make your own. This simple one was made of common pine and stained. Wrought brackets is another good idea.

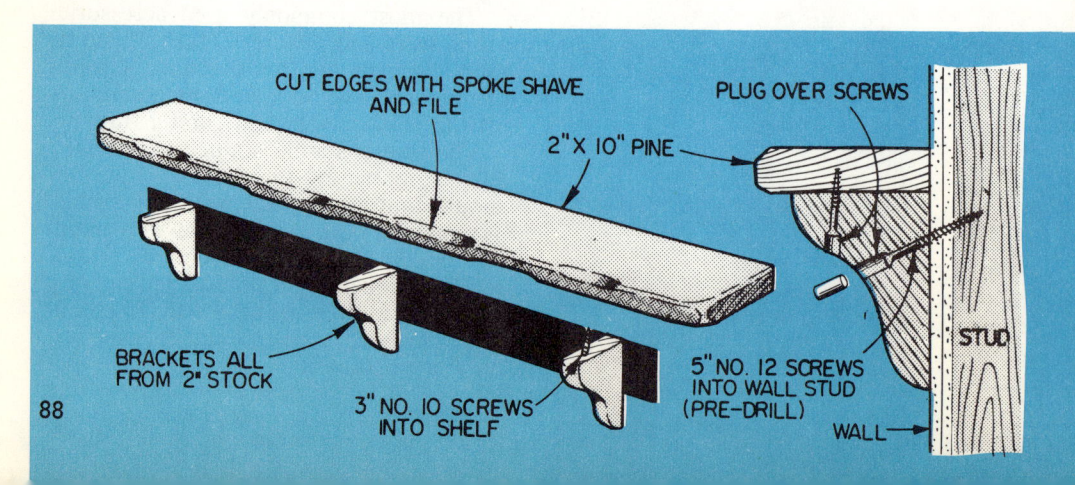

CUT EDGES WITH SPOKE SHAVE AND FILE
PLUG OVER SCREWS
2" X 10" PINE
BRACKETS ALL FROM 2" STOCK
3" NO. 10 SCREWS INTO SHELF
5" NO. 12 SCREWS INTO WALL STUD (PRE-DRILL)
STUD
WALL

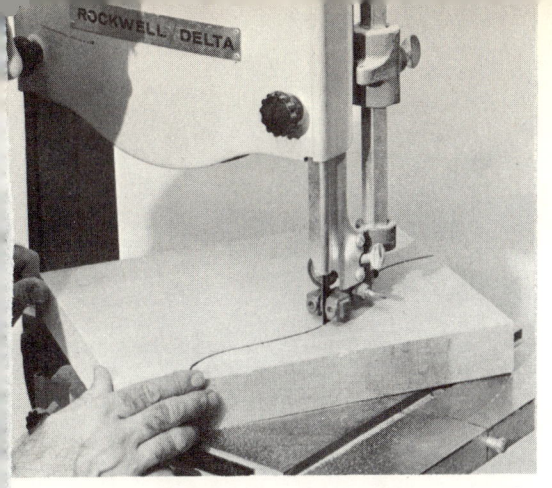

Thick shelf brackets are easily cut on the bandsaw. If not so equipped, you can use a saber saw or coping saw. For economy, building grade lumber will do a good job.

Shelf brackets are distressed using small gouge, "V" and straight chisels. Awl or nail can be used to make "worm" holes. Also strike wood with head or claw of hammer.

SHELVES

Shelves can line an entire wall for needed storage, or perhaps only a single shelf is all you need. You can use ready-made units or if you are handy you can make your own. Shelves can be massive Mediterranean masterpieces, or simple boards mounted on standards. They can be used as a mantle over a fireplace or placed low on a paneled wall as an accent piece.

Making a rough-hewn shelf is a simple project even for the amateur craftsman. Choose a suitable piece of lumber and shape the edges with a rasp or spokeshave. The rougher you make it, the better. A flat chisel can also be used. After the edges are shaped to your satisfaction, remove all splinters by using sandpaper. Do *not* sand

Child's wall-hung, boxlike curio cabinet is easily fashioned from scrap lumber. Decorative arched top is cut with sabre saw and is gaily painted with colorful sunflowers.

Cork wall makes a good background for lithograph and gear-shaped mirrors. The novelty drop lamp is fashioned like a light bulb. All are ideally suited for child's room.

Nothing frilly about this attic. Note how proper accessories create nautical air, and sturdy beams and rough-textured siding with the oak flooring breathe that Early Americana spirit.

until smooth, but only enough to remove the chips and splinters. Brackets are made of the same material except that they are not left as rough as the shelf. Cut the outline with a sabre saw, then round off the edges with a router or rasp.

If a more refined shelf is desired, sand the surfaces and edges as desired. Stain the shelf and brackets with a dark stain then finish with several coats of shellac or lacquer.

ACCENT WITH BEAMS

Beams are ideal for wall and ceiling decorations. They may be used for ornamental or structural purposes.

Here you have a choice of natural wood or *imitation beams* made of plastic foam or similar materials. *Wood beams* are either solid or boxed. Solid beams are very heavy and unless they are required structurally, most people prefer the box or plastic beams due to their lighterweight and ease of application.

Beams are used on ceilings, walls, over doorways, and around windows. They are also ideally used outdoors for a garden house or patio. Here, of course, real beams would be used.

Vertical beams on a wall can be used to break up the monotony of a large wall and likewise, high ceilings such as Cathedral ceilings, can be improved by use of beams.

Barclay

Dark shelving and beams to match are decorative and functional as well. Beams can be used to advantage when necessary to conceal joint between two wall coverings.

Marlite

All beams needn't be fancy or rough-hewn. The ones shown here are painted fir beams, used to separate kitchen and dining areas. Mural is a prefinished hardboard paneling.

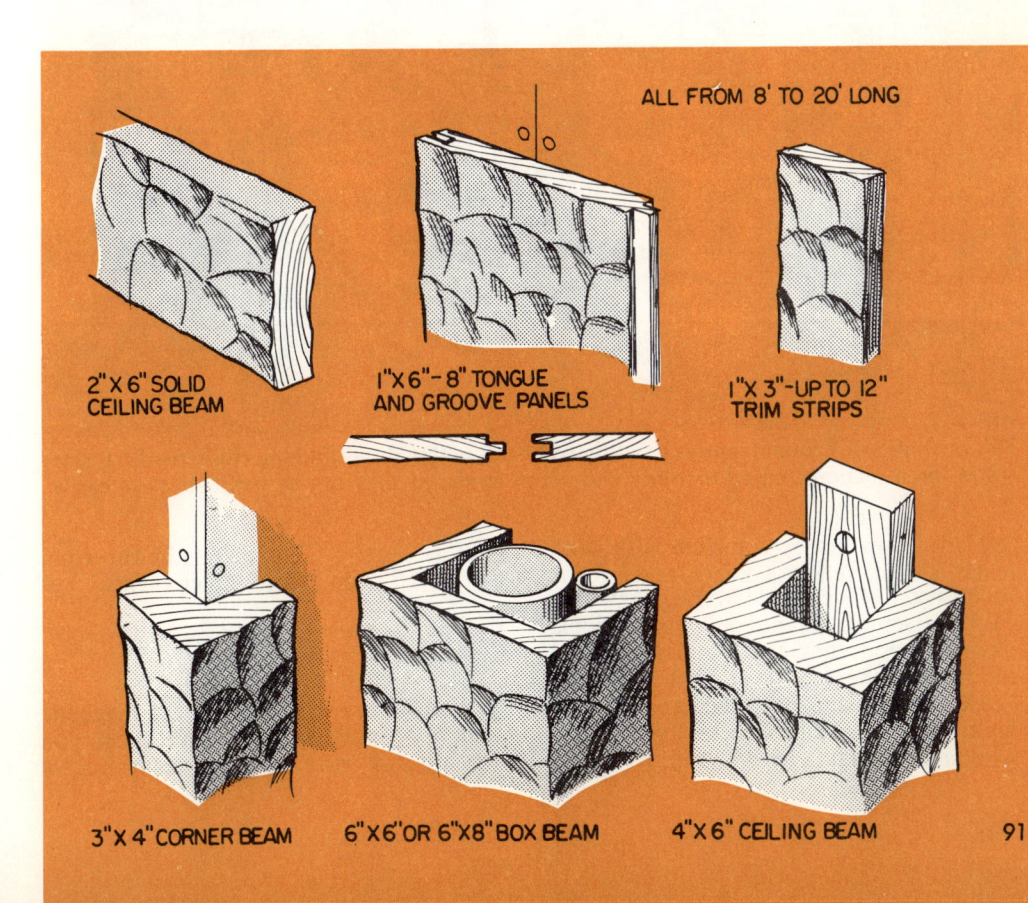

ALL FROM 8' TO 20' LONG

2" X 6" SOLID CEILING BEAM

1" X 6"-8" TONGUE AND GROOVE PANELS

1" X 3"-UP TO 12" TRIM STRIPS

3" X 4" CORNER BEAM

6" X 6" OR 6" X 8" BOX BEAM

4" X 6" CEILING BEAM

91

This country living room features hand-hewn beams with natural-looking chisel marks. Beams are in three sections, taped together with cloth strips, so they can be handled more easily.

Hand-hewn beams complete with adze marks are offered in a knock-down form unfinished. Made of plywood, they are easy to assemble and not only do they look like real wood, they are. Standard lumber fastened to the ceiling or wall acts as a "cleat." The beam is attached to this cleat with finishing nails. These beams are available in widths of 2" x 6", 4" x 6", 6" x 6", and 8" x 8". Lengths run from 8 ft. to 16 ft. in two-foot increments.

CURIO CABINETS

Wall hung curio cabinets are magnetic centers of interest in any room. Here you can display your favorite collection of

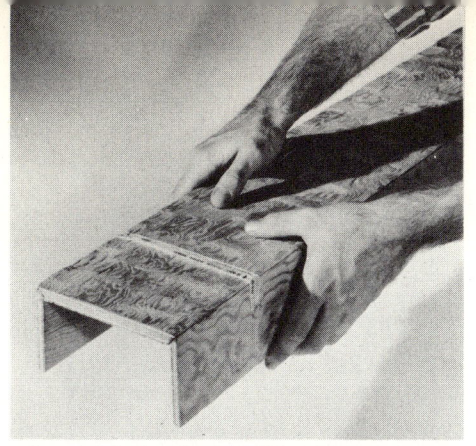

When folded with aid of hinged tape, beams form "U" channel which is nailed to previously installed 1"x6" nailer strip. Tape automatically spaces the three components.

With cloth tape hinge serving as a "third hand," beam sections are fastened at miter cuts by nailing 12" on center with 1" finishing nails. Tape is then removed; discard.

Lightweight beams are shipped and stored flat. Tape is removed after assembly. Beams are available at under $1.00 per ft. Lengths range from 8-ft. to 16-ft. in 2-ft. increments.

In final stage of installation, beam is raised to ceiling and placed open end over 1x6 nailer strip previously installed. One-inch finishing nails are placed at 16" intervals.

curios—birds, animals, figurines, etc. If your budget won't allow buying one, try your hand at making one. A simple version, suitable for a child's room is shown.

CLOCKS

Clocks are highly functional and decorative accessories. They come in so many traditional and modern styles, that you will easily find one suitable to your purposes. Many people however prefer to design and build their own and take much pleasure in this hobby.

You can purchase small battery-operated movements, cordless, and make your own clock cases. For a kitchen, you might use a ceramic dish or tile for the face. For a boy's room or den, you might cut out a ship or whale from wood, and use this as the clock face. These are suggestions and we have sketched a few more that might appeal to you. Why not try your own?

93

EARLY AMERICAN CLOCK

A timely gift project, the ideal wall accessory for kitchen or den

Easily made clock will add to the decor of any room. Make it from scrap wood, colorful buckram and clever battery powered movement. Makes a beautiful wall accent decoration.

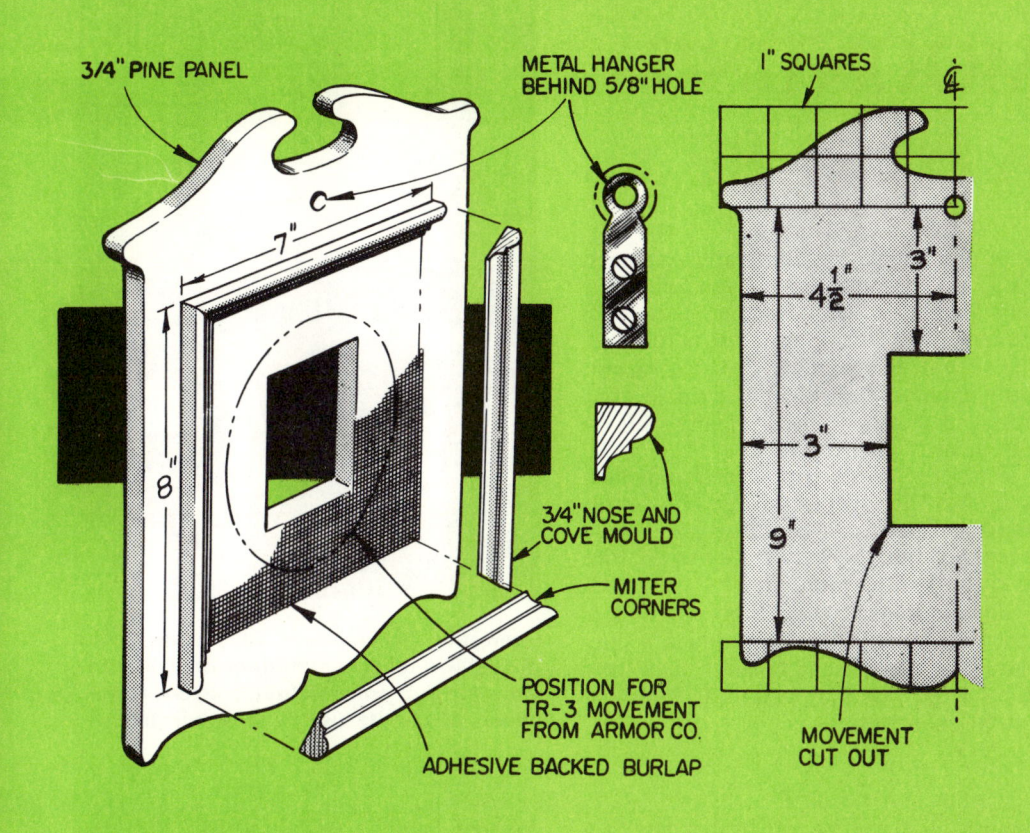

This distinctive Early American wall clock is easily made with scrap materials and a few basic tools. The clock is battery operated, thus eliminating dangling cords and outlet boxes.

PROCEDURES

The shape is cut from scrap lumber with a coping saw and the edges are rounded with sandpaper. If you have a saber saw and router, you can do the job faster but they are not really necessary.

An inner frame of pine molding adds dimension and interest to the clock face. To make the frame, use ¾" nose and cove molding which is sold at most lumber yards. Cut and miter the molding to size as shown, then assemble with brads and white glue.

An antique finish is then applied to the molding and outer framework. These finishes are available in kit form with easy to follow instructions, and come in a wide variety of colors, such as antique red, green or blue, or wood tones.

A colorful adhesive-backed burlap is used as background for the brass dial with glass bezel. Be sure to select a color that will harmonize with the antique finish that you have selected. For instance, a Chinese red burlap looks well with antique green finish or antique blue finish. Or, you may prefer a blue burlap with antique red finish. The adhesive-backed burlap is available at hardware shops and department stores. Simply cut to size, peel off backing, and press firmly into place.

Now attach the battery operated movement and brass dial, and it's done!

95

MOUNTING A PICTURE

Mounting photos, lithographs and posters, becomes easy if you follow the very simple technique shown here. Use ordinary wallpaper paste and hardboard. The slow drying paste is inexpensive but, more important, it will not wrinkle your print and it can be used equally well on light or heavy materials.

Tempered hardboard is recommended as it does not require sizing. The hardboard and print can be cut to size before mounting, but the better way is to trim them to size after mounting.

For unusual effects, thin plywood is bent into a soft curve to produce a contoured picture. The plywood can be held in a curved plane by nailing it to a contoured backboard.

Interesting arrangement of pictures over dining area relieves monotony of walls, provides topic of conversation, enlivens atmosphere. Also note use of wall mirror here.

Mitered joint can be cut by hand with a miter box and backsaw. Better way is to use table saw with miter gauge set at 45 degrees. Blade must be very sharp for a clean cut.

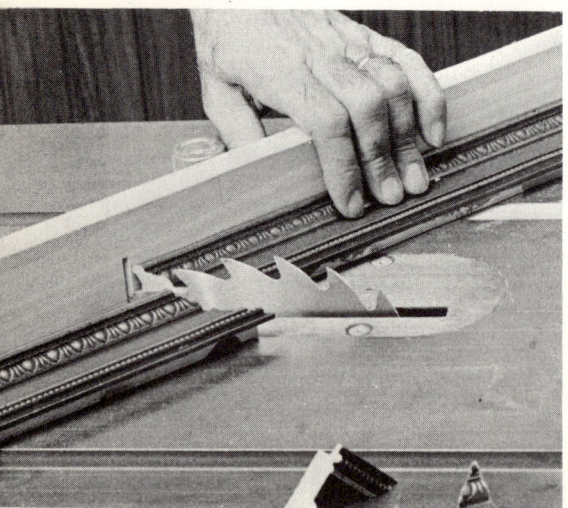

Mitered frame is assembled with glue and brads. For a strong joint, size the edge grain of the wood by using a thinned mixture of glue, allow to set, glue again; assemble.

Curved pictures are very dramatic and add depth to otherwise flat scene. The curve should be deeper at one end than the other. Try reverse curve with high spot at center.

Outer frame is made of ¾" wood. Vertical sections are beveled on one edge to match the contour of the curved pieces. Assemble with finishing nails and with white glue.

Use cardboard or thin plywood for the face of the frame. Bending gum plywood, ⅛" thick, is inexpensive and easy to use. Grain should run perpendicular to the curve.

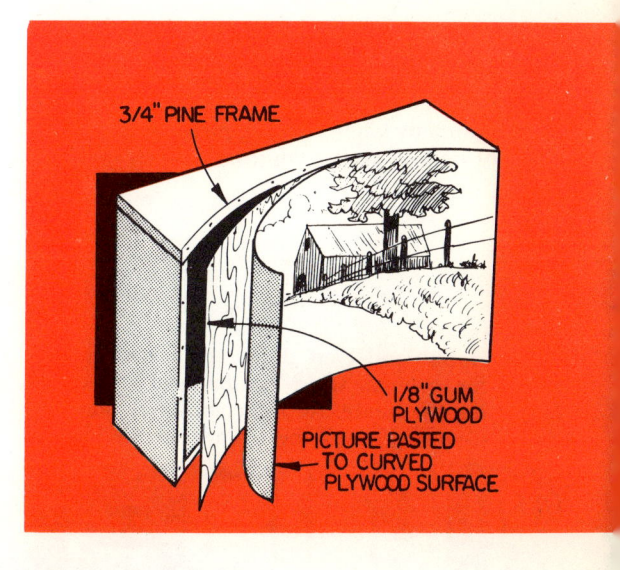

3/4" PINE FRAME
1/8" GUM PLYWOOD
PICTURE PASTED TO CURVED PLYWOOD SURFACE

Floral patterned wallpaper or vinyl hung in framed moldings is an excellent way to improve the appearance of a room, especially for large bare walls. Use nose and cove molding.

97

ACCENT WALLS

Accent walls can be created with carpet tiles. Use them to cover an entire wall, or just a small section if desired. The self-adhesive tiles are the easiest to install. Non-adhesive type can also be installed by using special double-face tape material mentioned earlier in this book. The wall must be free of all dust and dirt before application. If the wall is washed, be sure it is thoroughly dry.

Vibrating prints in this picture grouping prove it is no longer necessary to achieve symmetry when hanging pictures. Backdrop of cork as well as mirrors are self-sticking.

Hobby and craft shops are a great source for materials which can be used in decorating the home. All merchants welcome do-it-yourselfers; some even hold the classes.

Ceramic tiles are no longer limited to bathroom floors and shower stalls. They are more plentiful, more popular and more beautiful and have more uses than before.

Clever use of wallpaper shows what can be done with imagination. The triangular sections were cut with aid of straight edge and razor blade. Small pieces are easily installed.

Eye-catching wall of this bedroom can be easily duplicated. Table can be made or bought. Main attraction here is the use of white accessories against dark wall and rug.

This busy shelf is certainly earning its keep. Add-on units grow as your collection grows. Imposing shelf can be made to stretch completely across wall or you can tier them.
Barclay

Shag carpet squares are not only used wall-to-wall, they can even be used up a wall. Entire walls or accent strips are easily installed over any very clean dry surface.

Roxite

Screen dividers are the most widely used type. This is because they occupy little floor space, are easy to build or assemble, and are very effective in partitioning off almost any area.

TIPS ON DIVIDERS

Make them yourself or buy them to partition or enhance a room

Texture, design and function. Wrap these three decorating elements into a three-in-one package and you have a versatile tool for adding interest in many areas of the home.

Filigree hardboard is the versatile tool which holds an open sesame to charming, warm and inviting spots in the home that need "something" to give them life and interest.

As a room divider, a folding screen made with filigree hardboard shields as it allows passage of air and light. For these reasons, such a screen is popular in a recreation room, living room or bedroom. It affords privacy without unduly darkening the room.

A temporary room divider for the student's bedroom requires several 4x8-ft. filigree panels, framed with pre-grooved 1"x2" lumber, forming a divider that separates study from sleeping area, for example. When the student leaves home, the divider may be removed or relocated.

Room dividers like these are easy to construct. Lumber yards selling the per-

Roxite

Planter-type dividers are very popular, and can be made to hold real or artificial plants. For real plants, metal liner is required. This divider is plywood faced with fake stone.

Russ Stonier, Inc.

This unusual bamboo divider with an Oriental flair is made with wood turnings which are simply twisted together. Frame consists of 2x2 lumber with ¼" panels set in.

Infant's crib in corner of master bedroom has been separated by creating a room within a room using wallpaper, flooring, beams and dividers. Modular sections are useful.

An open divider of hardboard filigree separates dining and living rooms in this apartment. Light and air are not blocked, but areas are distinctly but quietly separated.

Roxite

forated hardboard normally have Masonite's pre-grooved moldings and accessories for assembling them. The thin, smooth panels simply slip into the grooves. Frames are glued and nailed.

In the case of the folding screen, hinges fasten the panels together.

The completed ensemble may be primed and painted to suit the location, using roller, brush or spray.

There are various other ways in which

101

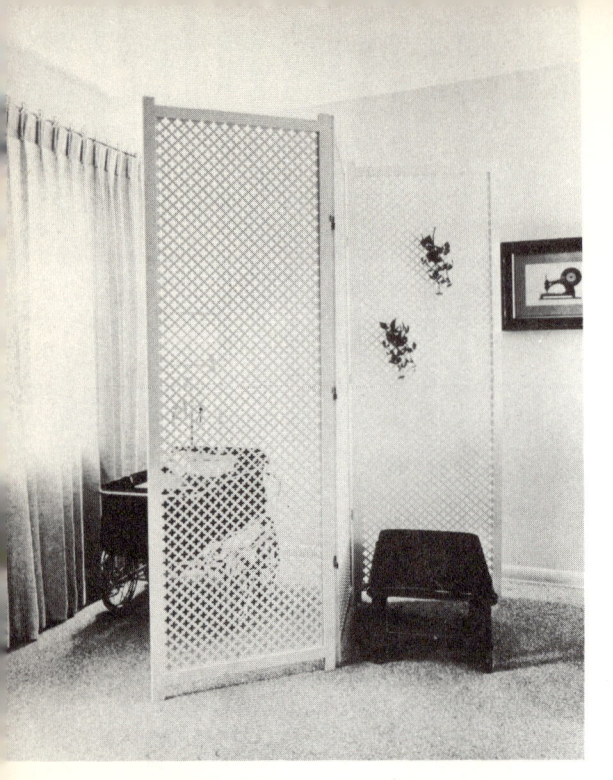

Folding screen of Masonite filigree with peek-through feature lets baby sleep undisturbed and with ample ventilation. Fitted moldings are available ready for assembly.

Divider unit blends in with textured walls, creates alcove for small piano. Frame, panel, and hardware are furnished in knock-down form. Height is adjustable. Assembly is easy.

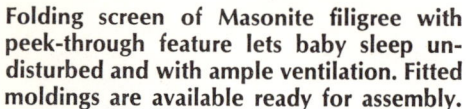

Barclay

Fabric-framed arch placed in corner sets off backlighted screen of filigree hardboard. Supported arch is made of ½" plywood and filigree screen is attached from the rear.
Masonite

filigree hardboard just ⅛" thick and smooth on both sides—can be used for texture, design and function in the home.

For example, the panels can be used in their natural deep brown or colorfully painted to spark interest as wall accents in any room in the home. Or they can be used as attractive inserts for interior shutters used on casement or double hung windows.

MORE USES FOR FILIGREE

An attractive closure for a bedroom storage wall could be a series of bifold doors with a filigree pattern. Or panels can be used in place of glass in construction of kitchen fixtures to cover fluorescent tubes or incandescent bulbs.

Stereo speaker grilles of this material can improve the appearance of the sound unit.

Simply arranging several pieces of fili-

Masonite

Ideal boys room boasts tough prefinished washable travertine hardboard paneling. Built-in shelves and desk are framed and edged with contrasting dark molding—for a lovely effect.

gree hardboard on a blank wall has merit, too. If framed, the rectangles can be used for mounting small paintings or other decorative objects. The frames permit insertion of hooks to hold these objects in place.

The craftsman working with filigree may find it easier to prime and paint, or stain, the individual pieces before assembling. This suggestion extends to the framing, which may be given the same or a contrasting finish.

ROOM DIVIDER GIVES PRIVACY PLUS STUDY, HOBBY SPACE

In a boy's room, space needed for a single bed is minimal. To partially screen the bed, build a floor-to-ceiling divider about 18" away.

Face each side with perforated hardboard, so the boy will have clothes hanging space on the bed side and a study area on the room side.

Build a counter two feet wide and 5 or 6 ft. long at desk height (30" or 31") and he'll have a wonderful place for study and hobbies. Shelves and hooks on the perforated hardboard above will provide ample room for books, pictures, pennants and the like.

The alcove formed by the divider for the single bed can be made practically carefree, too, by installation of prefinished paneling available in a variety of woodgrains, textures and colors. This durable paneling wipes clean with a damp cloth.

Add some lighting fixtures to both sides of the room divider, and the young man will be nicely equipped to make excellent use of his bedroom for sleep, study or hobbies.

Carpeting offers an acoustical quality that will help make the room a quiet retreat.

ROSETTE

CLOVERLEAF

CAMELOT

REGENCY

CEILINGS

FOLDING SCREENS

FURNITURE GRILLES

BI-FOLD DOORS

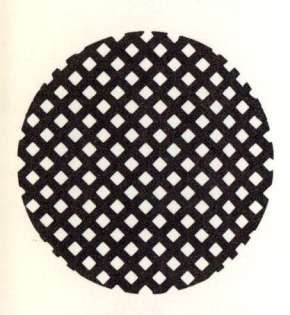

ROOM DIVIDERS

BUILT-IN GRILLES

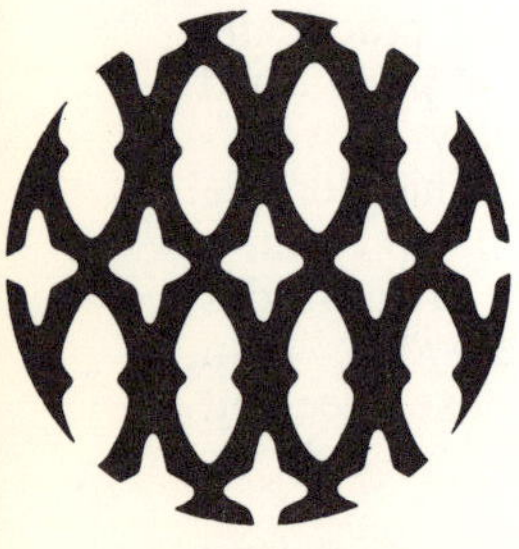

SPEAKER GRILLES

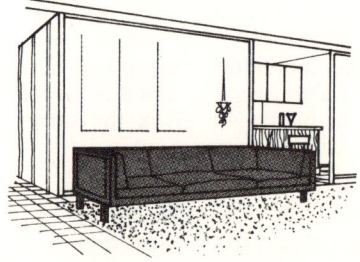

WALL ACCENTS

In addition to their use for dividers, filigree panels can be put to work in other areas around the house. Open pattern of design permits ventilation without obstructing light and movement. Pattern adds interest.

Combination art gallery and room divider was made with pre-grooved lumber. Spring tension and glide assemblies render the unit removable. Use lumber for more permancy.

Instead of louvers, these doors concealing vanity feature hardboard filigree panels. Same setup can be used to construct folding screens by joining the sections with hinges.

Masonite Corp.

Other versatile applications of filigree paneling are shown here. The sliding bookcase doors and the matching window cornice utilize the same attractive filigree pattern.

Wood is the warmest and most beautiful material for windows. A lot has been done to keep them modern, durable, and easy to maintain, such as better preservatives, and new designs.

WHY WOOD WINDOWS

Read this carefully if you are thinking of building or remodeling

Ask any woman why she prefers wood windows and she will undoubtedly point out first their *attractive appearance*. Compare any wood window with a metal window and you will be comparing warmth and color to cold uninviting metal. Not much competition there.

Wood windows come in so many styles and sizes—bow, bay, round, octagonal, casement, awning, etc.—and can be stained or painted in so many wonderful colors that they are an exciting stimulant to a woman's decorating skill. On the basis of beauty, nothing beats wood.

THE PRACTICAL POINTS

On the other hand, if you ask a man why he prefers wood windows he will point to many more practical and economical reasons. For instance, wood windows have much *better insulating protection* against heat and cold, and there is *less of a moisture condensation* problem. This means a savings in fuel bills and air conditioning costs.

Humidity is essential and beneficial in the home since it keeps plaster from cracking, prevents wallpaper from peeling,

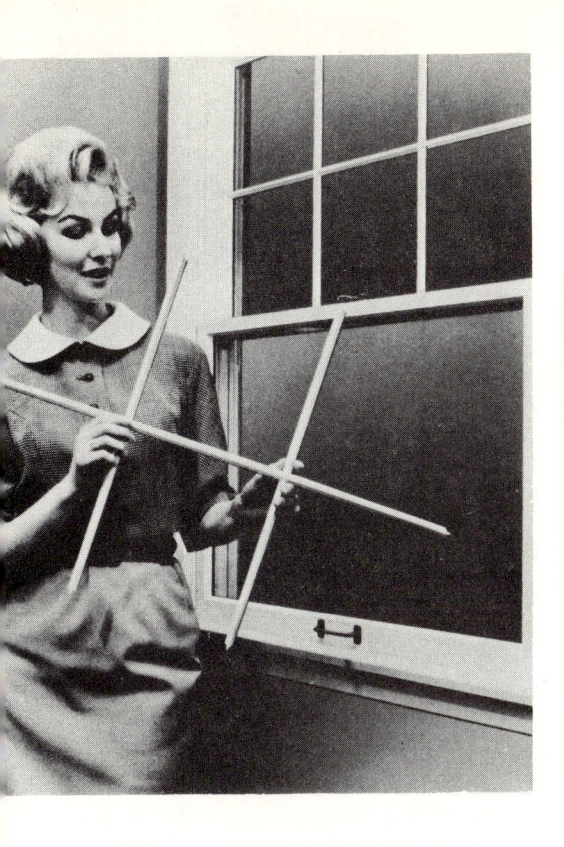

Removable grilles of ponderosa pine or vinyl for windows are a welcome innovation for any homeowner. Snap-in, snap-out grilles add to appearance, washing is easier.

The most common styles of removable grilles are shown below, left to right—Modern (horizontal), Colonial (diamond), and Traditional (rectangular). Choice is yours.

Removable wood grilles, made to fit all windows, greatly simplify painting and washing. New Mediterranean style shown, ponderosa pine, fits casement windows from 24" to 72" tall.

This mediterranean style wood grille blends window and grille as a single unit. Available in natural wood, they can be stained or painted to match the beauty of your room.

Removable grilles are among the modern low-maintenance features available in wood window units. They snap out to simplify window washing. Window is one pane.

keeps people more comfortable with less drying of skin and respiratory passages. But excess humidity will cause water condensation and moisture can form on window sashes and run down on carpeting and walls, causing a messy and expensive problem.

ABOUT THE NEW WOOD WINDOWS

New wood windows are *water-repellent* and *preservative treated* against termites and decay. *Factory weatherstripping* makes the windows more airtight and better insulators. *New designs* in windows make them much easier to wash.

A new type of window now on the market combines the advantages of wood windows plus the advantage of a vinyl coating on the exposed exterior surfaces. Whereas the inner wood parts can be stained or painted, all exterior parts have a vinyl shield that won't warp, rust or pit and does not require painting or maintenance. All this plus a vinyl weather stripping makes for an ideal window.

Removable grilles made of ponderosa pine wood or vinyl are available for stock wood windows at local lumber dealers. They snap in or out easily and can be readily removed for window washing or painting.

They also add beauty and dimension to windows and are available in four styles to fit your room decor, octagonal and diamond for traditional and colonial homes, horizontal for modern homes, and Mediterranean for Spanish type homes. They greatly improve the exterior and interior appearance of the home.

Marlite

This master bathroom sports a luxurious look plus easy maintenance. Prefinished plastic-coated paneling can be damp wiped to clean and is resistant to heat, moisture and to stains.

NEW FOR THE BATHROOM

Modern innovations that make upkeep easy

It's a mod, mod world with the new One Piece Bathing Suite made by the Formica Corporation of Cincinnati, Ohio. This module is molded of colorfast Acrylite acrylic sheet, the same material used as windows on supersonic aircraft.

This is the only bathing module we know of with one step installation. It is seamless and cornerless, has no tile joints, cracks or crevices to collect dirt or mold. The module is available in three models— 60" tub & shower combination, 48" shower, and 36" shower. The one-piece bathing suite has an integral top as well as walls and tub, and includes molded shelves and seat. All modules have slip-resistant floor for added safety. The module is available in white and four colors— beige, blue, gold and avocado.

Once installed, there are no redecorating problems. There will be no peeling paint or wallpaper problems. The module is colorfast, durable and easily cleaned. Sliding tempered glass enclosures and mobile shower heads are optional accessories.

REVAMP THAT OLD BATHROOM

Another bathroom renewal project for the do-it-yourselfer is ideal for an older bath where the walls are in poor condition and need to be completely covered but one wishes to keep the tub. The Swan Corporation of St. Louis, Mo., offers a Fiberglas tub-surround called Tubwal. This is a 3-panel unit which is intended for finish-

Formica Corp.

One-piece, molded acrylic shower module is seamless and cornerless. No more messy grout to contend with and cleaning is a pleasure. Combined shower-tub is available.

Formica Corp.

New non-metallic all-plastic shower cabinet is available through plumbing dealers. Ideally suited for use in new or remodeled basements, attics, and even for mobile homes.

ing the walls above a standard-size tub and which eliminates need for grouting, painting or edge moldings.

The two side pieces are 58" high and extend around the corners to form part of the covering of the back center wall. Therefore there is no troublesome corner joint. The center component overlaps over these two pieces on the back wall. Cutting is required only where plumbing fixtures come through or where windows obstruct.

To install, special mastic is applied to the backs of the Fiberglas panels to insure a permanent bond. A pressure sensitive tape is factory installed around the edges of the 3 components to seal and hold the tub-surround to the wall until the mastic is cured completely. Special sealant is applied to joints along edge of tub and around top edges of the panels. The fin-

Carefully mark exact location for plumbing outlets on Fiberglas panels. Use a drill or table saw to cut out holes for fixtures, window, lightswitches, etc. Do this with care.

Apply special mastic to the back of the Fiberglas panels and around cutout holes. Remove protective backing from pressure sensitive tape to expose adhesive surface.

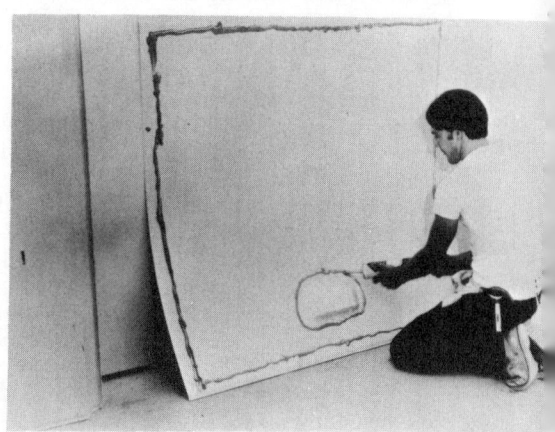

The Swan Corp.

Press the two side panels firmly in place against old wall. Then apply third overlapping back section. Now apply special sealant along tub edge and around top edges.

ished Tubwal is smooth, durable, and easily cleaned.

PANELING FOR THE BATHROOM

Although Formica laminate paneling has been around for a long time and proved its worth, the new Panel System 202 has even more advantages to offer and is highly recommended for installa-

First step in installation of "Panel System 202" is to measure and layout all base moldings. Nail moldings into position. To apply over the tiles, use the adhesive activator.

Formica Corp.

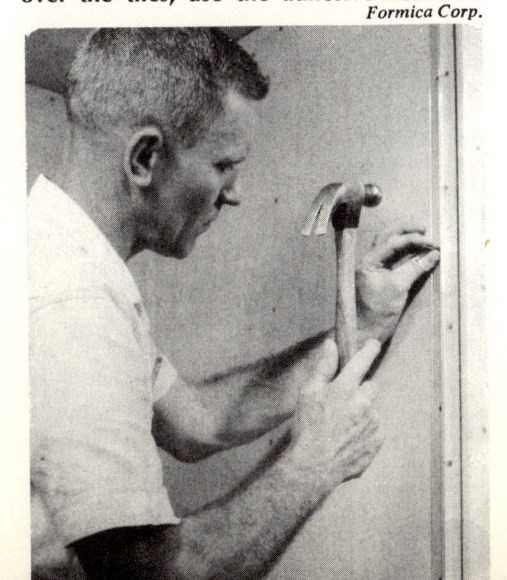

The Swan Corp.

When finished the Tubwal is smooth, gleaming, easily cleaned and durable. It is available in six popular decorator colors. No moldings are needed for this project.

tion in high humidity areas such as bathrooms and kitchens. The panels have a polystyrene core which will absorb the irregularities of the wall surface to which it is applied. The panels can be installed over existing tile walls, masonry walls, plaster walls or any other sound, reasonably smooth wall surface. A new one-coat adhesive system instead of contact cement reduces installation time.

Make all cutouts. Cut panels to shape. "Dry fit" panels to assure good fit. Use paper templates to assure accurate cut, fit and proper alignment, these are all important.

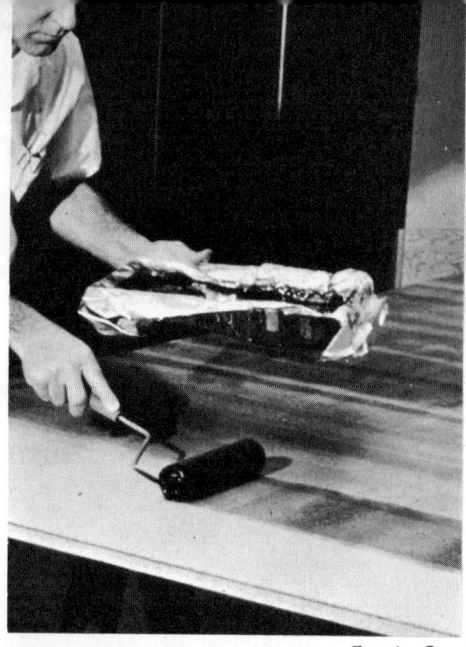

Apply liberal coating of adhesive activator to perimeter of wall area to be covered. Use mohair paint roller, not a brush. Remove protective backing and apply activator.

Formica Corp.

With panel in position, apply firm pressure to entire panel with rubber J-roller or wood block and hammer to assure a uniform contact cement bond which is so important.

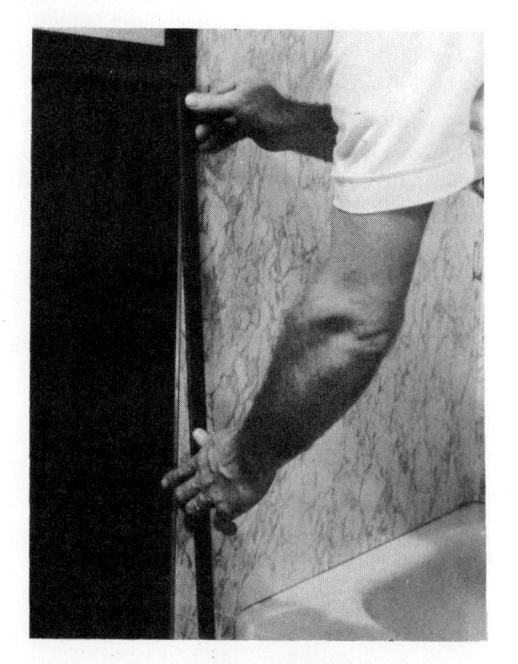

Apply decorative face moldings, horizontal first then vertical ones. Tap into place with wood block. Seal all panel edges with Dow 780 sealant and the job is complete.

Formica Corp.

The system is available in a wide range of colors, designs and woodgrains. The system produces a smooth surface with no grout lines, no chipping, no place for dirt or mildew. It resists moisture, it is durable and easily cleaned.

Panels come in five sizes and are factory coated with adhesive in a non-active state to assure proper adhesion and coverage. After cutting and fitting the panels, an adhesive activator is applied with a roller. Put into place by applying pressure all over with J-roller or wood block and hammer.

A free-standing cabinet unit can be made with ready-made turned spindles, some shelving and some imagination. The remarkable feature here is that no glue is required in assembly.

CREATE WITH SPINDLES

Here's a quick and easy way to make many useful items without tools

The creative possibilities when using ready-made turned spindles are unlimited. Hardwood spindles turned to perfection are available in about a half dozen styles and lengths.

Connectors both rigid and flexible make numerous lengths possible. The flexible connector permits floor to ceiling poles formed with the spindles to be snapped into position.

Russ Stonier, Inc.

Spindles are turning up everywhere in the home. Bedroom, kitchen and parlor are likely places you'll see them. Assembled without glue, they can be taken apart with ease.

This attractive server was made with a variety of spindles. If you own a lathe, you can turn any of the shapes shown. Wood used should be hard variety, e.g. maple or birch.

Shelving is available both regular and notched, for building double-length units. The fact that the *shelves and other assemblies go together without tools, screws, or glue,* has made them very popular among remodelers and decorators. Parts may be purchased individually or in kit form. Some kits include antiquing materials.

A recent newcomer in the field of spindles is a similar product made with all components molded of plastic and prefinished.

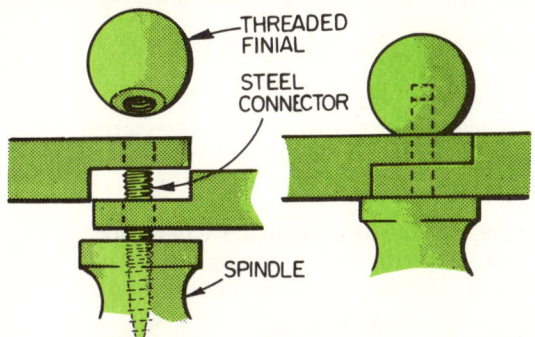

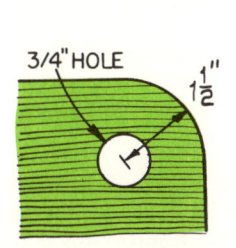

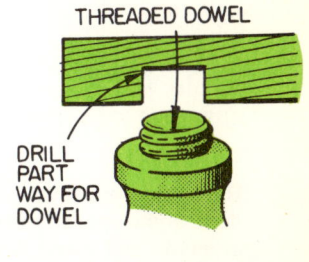

THREADED FINIAL
STEEL CONNECTOR
SPINDLE
3/4" HOLE
1½"
THREADED DOWEL
DRILL PART WAY FOR DOWEL

These photos illustrate just a few of the many furniture possibilities using ready-made turned spindles. Hardwood parts include finials, threaded dowels, spacers. Potential is unlimited.

DECORATING WITH TAPE

Design unusual accent pieces with foil and plastic tapes

Pressure-sensitive tapes are being used more and more around the house for decorating, repairing and other jobs. Some are plastic, some paper, some cloth. Some are adhesive-backed on one side only, some on both sides.

They are referred to as "pressure-sensitive" because they already have an adhesive substance applied and need only be pressed firmly into place. They are especially good for decorating purposes since they can be easily removed and changed and rarely leave any adhesive residue behind.

It is important that the surface be clean and dry before applying the pressure sensitive tape so be sure to wipe off the surface with detergent before any application. Let dry.

Double-faced tapes are especially useful for such decorating projects as applying fringe trims to cornices or shades. They can also be used for hanging posters or lightweight pictures, for laying tiles, to cover a wall or headboard with fabric, etc. The tape is 1½" wide and comes in rolls. It is almost indispensable to have around as an all-purpose household and decorating tape.

MAKING BOUTIQUE ITEMS

A new foil craft kit by Arno is available for creating beautiful boutique accessories. This kit contains gold-colored foil tape and

Four easy steps transform a piece of pressure-sensitive foil tape into an attractive decorative item. Stylus is used to emboss the tape on the backside. When protective backing is removed, a deeply embossed design results. This is applied to a suitable object—for instant beauty.

Picture frames can be improved by application of foil tape. Combination of foil and plastic tape was used in top frame for an unusual effect. Repeat designs can be made.

Three fine examples of what can be accomplished with foil tape. Box at top was antiqued and burnished to bring out highlights. Designs are taken from compacts, etc.

aluminum foil tape, both 2" wide, plus four embossing patterns and an embossing stylus with instruction booklet. The tape can be used to decorate picture frames, jewelry boxes, canisters, etc. Since it is also waterproof, it can be used on outdoor items too.

For dimensional design, to cover an object, such as a picture frame, pull the backing strip slowly away from the foil as you apply tape, shiny side up, an inch or two at a time. Rub the entire surface with the stylus until the pattern is well defined.

To emboss a design, cut the length of tape needed; leave the blue backing strip on.

● Select a pattern from the kit or any 1/8" deep pattern around the house, position the tape over the pattern, foil side down, and tape in position.

● Press the tape down firmly on the pattern, then with the stylus and working on the blue backing strip, rub all areas carefully. *Do not puncture the foil.*

● Lift the tape off pattern and pull backing strip carefully away from the foil.

● Finally apply the embossed foil tape strip to the object to be decorated; trim corners and edges with a razor blade.

Incidentally, the *aluminum foil tape,* since it *is airtight, watertight and conforms to any shape without breaking,* has many valuable repair uses. It can be used for wrapping exhaust pipes and mufflers, leaky downspouts, and other metal surface repairs. It's great also for decorative and trimming jobs around the house.

Embossed tape was used to cover this wood box, but cardboard and plastic boxes will do as well. When surface being covered is wider than tape, edges of strips are butted.

Photos from
Arno Adhesive Tapes, Inc.

This elegant table can be made with readily available materials. Fir plywood has been covered with scraps of paneling. The top and edges are covered with black slate plastic laminate.

BUILD A COFFEE TABLE

Make it from prefinished materials, without power tools

This lovely table can be easily put together using leftover paneling, decorative appliques, and slate surfaced plastic laminate. *Power tools are handy but not essential.*

The main members of the table are made of plywood then covered with the paneling. Except for touching up the applique, the *table will not require finishing* if the paneling used is the prefinished type. The laminated top needs no finishing and even the molding used can be prefinished.

HOW TO BUILD

• Choose a good flat piece of plywood for the top. Cut it to size then build up the edges by adding a 1½" wide strip all around.

• Assemble with glue and 1¼" nails. Drive the nails from the bottom side. Be certain that the *edges are perfectly aligned.* Nail heads are sunk using a nail set.

• Next, build the base, again using ¾" plywood. Add the floor pieces using glue and 2" finishing nails.

• Now select four pieces of paneling and cut widths ½" wider than the plywood uprights.

• Miter the sides using a tablesaw or block plane. (The height of the panels should be the same as the uprights.)

• Mount the panels to one side of the uprights, using brads and glue. Place the brads along the base where they will be covered by the molding, later.

• Also place them along the top where they will be concealed by the apron. White glue is recommended.

• Cut the apron to size and add the panel facing. Align the pieces and assemble the partially covered uprights to the

Coat entire surface of boards with glue. Spread in wavy pattern as shown, then brush out to cover entire area evenly. Follow same procedure when coating the paneling.

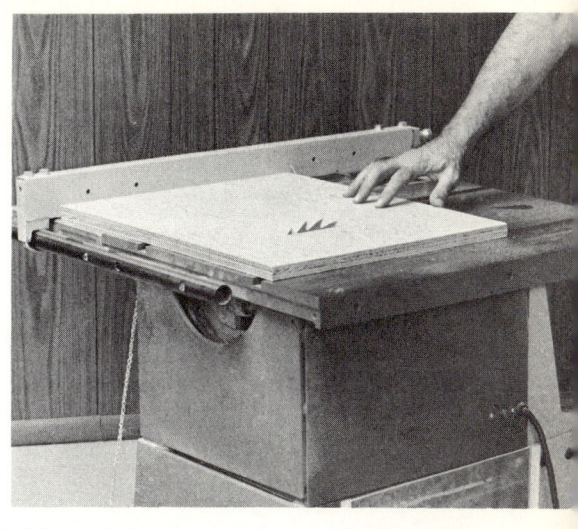

Table uprights are cut from ¾" plywood. Set fence of saw to cut all the widths at one time. Since boards will be covered, you can use low grade plywood, but it must be flat.

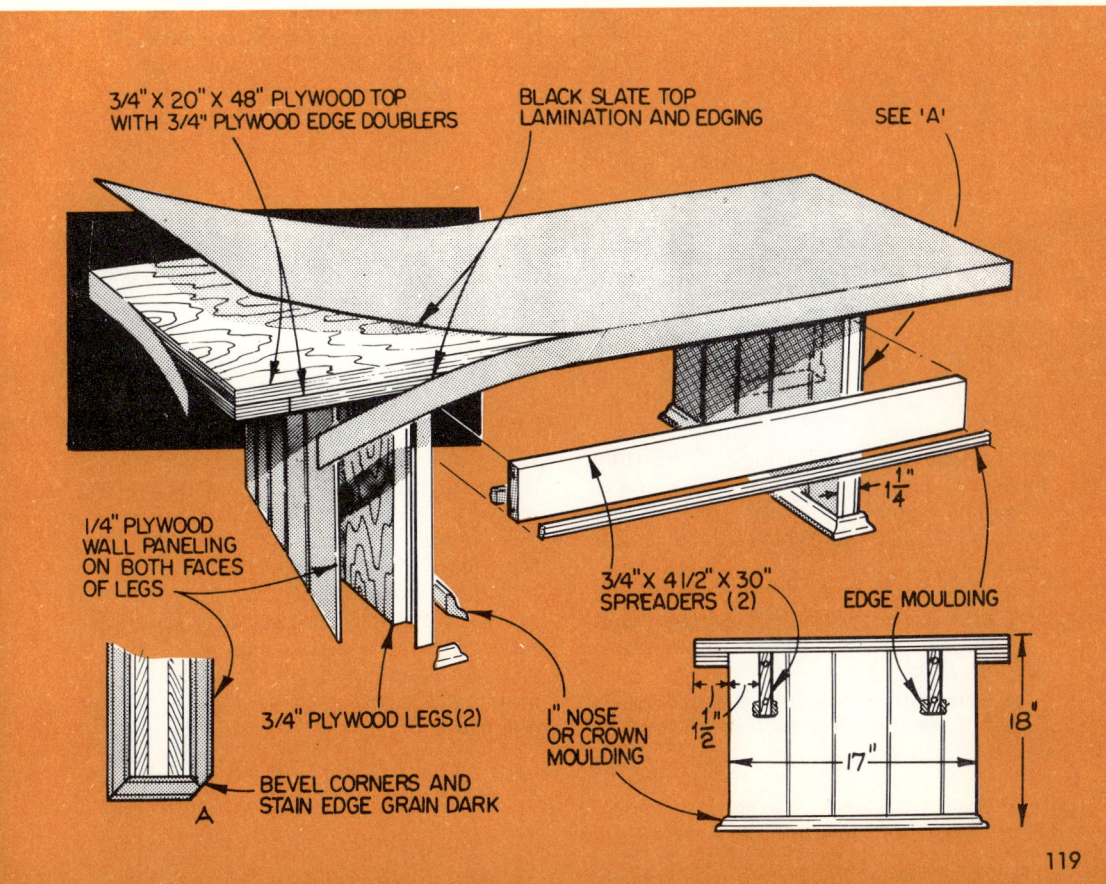

3/4" X 20" X 48" PLYWOOD TOP WITH 3/4" PLYWOOD EDGE DOUBLERS

BLACK SLATE TOP LAMINATION AND EDGING

SEE 'A'

1/4" PLYWOOD WALL PANELING ON BOTH FACES OF LEGS

3/4" X 4 1/2" X 30" SPREADERS (2)

EDGE MOULDING

3/4" PLYWOOD LEGS (2)

1" NOSE OR CROWN MOULDING

BEVEL CORNERS AND STAIN EDGE GRAIN DARK

1 1/2"

17"

18"

1 1/4"

119

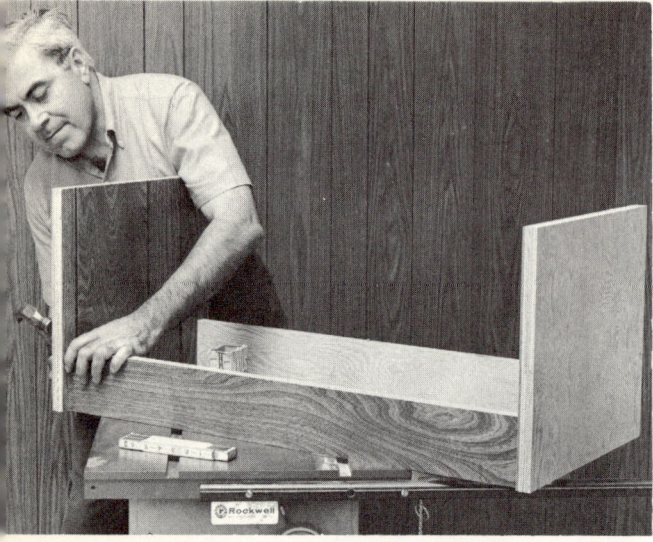

Table is assembled in stages. Ends are nailed to apron before face piece is applied. Scrape away finish in area where apron contacts end panel. Glue and nail to secure.

Final assembly consists of adding outer panels and edge pieces. Hold the panels in place with brads driven where they can be covered with molding. Clamps are helpful.

two apron sections, using 2" finishing nails.
- The remaining panels are now assembled to the uprights and the edge pieces added.
- Coat all mating surfaces with glue and wipe any squeeze-out that may result. Moldings at base and lower edge of apron may be added now.
- The laminate is now applied to the edges of the top. (See section on working with laminates elsewhere in this book.) If a rigid laminate is used, you will probably need a router to trim it.
- When the edges have been laminated, but before the top laminate is applied, locate the top on the base section and nail or screw firmly. The fasteners should be set a trifle below the surface.
- Add laminate to the top, trim to size, and fasten applique. Your table is now complete!

Not all moldings are used on doors or walls. Clever use of ordinary stock moldings were used to build this attractive cabinet. Nose and cove molding was used at cabinet's top edge.

INSTANT MAGIC

Make quick transformations using moldings, carvings and trims

You can magically transform simple unadorned walls and furniture by adding decorative moldings, carvings or other trims.

BORDERS FOR ACCENT

Borders of either wallpaper or fabric can be practical as well as decorative. They will cover uneven or poorly trimmed wallpaper edgings near ceilings and doors.

They will brighten, add interest, and a professional finish to otherwise plain painted walls. They can also be utilized as chair rails, wall panels, and door frames. They are also ideally suited for decorating lamp shades, room dividers, screens, valances, window shades, etc.

Installation of the borders is easy. Any wallpaper paste may be used and three types of joints are involved—the diagonal-butt, the miter, and the dart for forming a "T" joint. The tools required for this

Moldings can be used to create interesting effects. Here a crown molding forms base.

Greek key molding is available in various sizes, some are carved others pressed out.

unique decorating material are a straight edge, razor blade, small brush and a sponge.

Cut the border to size and locate before applying the paste. Light pencil marks can be used to locate the strips. Apply the paste to the back of the strip using a brush 2½" wide. Let the paste set for a few minutes then hang the strip using a damp sponge to work out any air bubbles.

MOLDINGS FOR HIGHLIGHTS

Wood moldings are the most versatile of decorating materials. In addition to their usual uses around doors, ceilings and floors, they can be put to work in many fascinating ways. Some uses are shown on these pages, but you can probably think of many more.

Moldings are available in many forms. They may be purchased unfinished, prefinished, vinyl clad or molded of plastic or pressed wood. They can also be made by the homecraftsman equipped with the necessary tools.

Used vertically, molding will make a room appear taller. Horizontally, they will make a short room seem longer.

Around windows they can be made to conceal curtain rods and curtain tops. A plain door can be transformed dramatically by the addition of moldings. Kitchen cabinets can be updated by adding moldings, new hardware and a coat of paint. Antiquing is especially attractive on cabinets trimmed with moldings.

Plain chests are a favorite for the molding-conscious do-it-yourselfers. Drawer fronts can be paneled with plain or fancy moldings. Molding can also be applied to the sides. If the top of a chest has a plain edge, a strip of nose and cove molding will do wonders for it.

COMBINE MOLDINGS AND WALL COVERINGS

You can combine moldings and fabrics or wallpapers effectively on walls or cabinets. Simply frame out panels with molding, then insert the fabric or self-adhesive plastic or paper within the paneled area. Fabrics can be applied with paste or glue. The new spray-type adhesives work very well especially on fabrics.

You'll find that working with moldings is not at all difficult. Joints are either mitered, coped or butted. Outside corners are always mitered, and inside corners may be

Make raised panels with picture frame molding. Glue on beveled center piece to finish.

With help of ready-made moldings, a novice can make simple but attractive furniture.

either mitered or coped. The coped joint is best for inside corners. This is one in which the end of the molding is shaped to match the face of the adjacent piece. The technique calls for making a back-hand miter then cutting with a coping saw the shape left by the reverse miter.

Room trim moldings are generally held with nails, but small moldings as used on cabinets and similar projects, can be installed with brads or glue. If glue is used, the area under the moldings must be free of paint or other finish.

INSTANT ELEGANCE

Carvings and appliques make for instant elegance. They can be used on walls, doors, cabinets or even ceilings. They are available in various forms—pressed wood, molded plastic, carved wood, stamped metal and cast metal.

The carvings can be used by themselves or in conjunction with moldings to form interesting patterns. A cluster of carvings mounted on the ceiling around a chandelier can be breathtaking. Unpainted furniture worked over with carvings and moldings can be made to look like an expensive piece.

Ethan Allen

You can use wood moldings in many ways. Here they are used to create panel accents. You can carry this idea further by placing your favorite fabric or wallpaper in frame.

123

LIST OF SOURCES FOR MATERIALS

Most of the materials mentioned in this book are available locally at lumberyards and building supply dealers and paint and hardware shops. You will also find a good deal of material at large department stores and the mail order houses.

If you should have difficulty in locating a particular item locally, or if you desire further information or literature, you may write to the Consumer Relations department of the firms listed.

SOURCE	MATERIALS
American Olean Tile Co. Lansdale, Pa. 19446	ceramic tiles
American Plywood Assoc. 1119 "A" Street Tacoma, Wash. 98401	moldings, plywood & paneling
Amerock Corp. 4000 Auburn St. Rockford, Ill. 61101	cabinet hardware
Armor Company, Inc. Box 290 Deer Park, N.Y. 11729	clock movements, casters & hardware
Armstrong Cork Co. Lancaster, Pa. 17604	flooring tiles, carpeting, ceiling tiles
Arno Tapes Box 301 Michigan City, Ind. 46360	adhesive tapes
Bangkok Industries 1900 S. 20 St. Philadelphia, Pa. 19145	wood flooring
Barclay Industries 65 Industrial Rd Lodi, N.J. 07644	wood paneling, moldings, adhesives
Black & Decker Towson, Maryland	power tools
John Boos & Co. 315 South First St. Effingham, Ill. 62401	maple chopping blocks
Borden Co. 350 Madison Ave. New York, N.Y. 10017	glues
Conso Products 27 W. 23 St. New York, N.Y. 10010	trimmings, pleater tape
Dacor Mfg. Co. 65 Armory St. Worcester, Mass. 01601	artificial stone, brick
Evans Products Co. 1121 S.W. Salmon St. Portland, Oregon 97208	building materials, paneling
Formica Corp. 120 E. 4th St. Cincinnati, Ohio	plastic laminates & bathroom paneling
General Bathroom Products 2201 Touhy Ave. Elk Grove, Village, Ill. 60007	bathroom products
Georgia-Pacific 900 S.W. Fifth Ave. Portland, Oregon 97204	paneling, moldings
The Meyercord Co. 365 E. North Ave. Carol Stream, Ill. 60187	decals
Millers Falls Co. 57 Wells Greenfield, Mass, 01301	tools
Minnesota Mining & Mfg. Co. St. Paul, Minn.	glues & spray adhesives
Montgomery Ward & Co. Branches in almost all cities	all home-improvement items
Morgan Adhesives Co. 4560 Darrow Rd. Stowe, Ohio 44224	self-adhesive products
Morgan Company Box 530 Oshkosh, Wisc. 54901	doors
Red Cedar Shingle Bureau 5510 White Bldg. Seattle, Wash.	cedar shakes
Rockwell Mfg. Co. 400 No. Lexington Ave. Pittsburgh, Pa. 15208	power tools & stationary tools
Gold Bond Building Products 325 Delaware Ave. Buffalo, N.Y. 14202	building materials
Illinois Bronze Powder & Paint Co. Lake Zurich, Ill. 62047	creative paint products
Kentile 58 Second Ave. Brooklyn, N.Y. 11215	floor tiles
Ozite Corp. 1755 Butterfield Rd. Libertyville, Ill. 60048	shag carpeting & self-stick carpeting
Macklanburg Duncan Co. Box 25188 Oklahoma City Okla. 73125	drawer glides, builders hardware
Majestic Co. 733 Erie Huntington, Ind. 46750	fireplaces
Marlite Co. Dover, Ohio 44622	Marlite panels
Masonite Corp. 29 N. Wacker Drive Chicago, Ill. 60606	filigree panels, hardboard, paneling
Rohm & Haas Independence Mall West Philadelphia, Pa. 19105	Plexiglas
Roseburg Lumber Co. Box 1088 Roseburg, Oregon 97470	moldings, paneling
Roxite Division Masonite Corp. 7800 North Milwaukee Ave. Niles, Ill. 60648	decorator panels
Sears Roebuck & Co. Branches in most cities	all home-improvement items
Stanley Works New Britain, Conn.	hand tools, power tools & hardware
Stauffer Chemical Co. Westport, Conn. 06880	laminated shades
Russ Stonier Inc. Chicago, Ill. 60654	spindles
The Swan Corp. St. Louis, Mo.	bathroom panels
Richard Thibaut, Inc. Box 1541 G.P.O. New York, N.Y. 10001	wallcoverings
U.S. Plywood 777 Third Ave. New York, N.Y.	moldings, paneling, plywood & glue
Wallpaper Information Bureau 969 Third Ave. New York, N.Y. 10022	wallpapers
Western Wood Products Assoc. 1500 Yeon Bldg. Portland, Oregon 97204	paneling, moldings, lumber
Window Shade Manufacturers Assoc. 230 Park Ave. New York, N.Y. 10017	window shades

INDEX

Index Key:
Chapter heads are in capital letters
Bold face numerals indicate a photo
Italicized numerals indicate diagram

A

abrasives, 19
ACCENT WALLS, 98
acclimating panels, **8**
acoustical tiles, **70**
adhesive, 14
adhesive activator, **112**
adhesive, latex type, 50
adhesive mortar, 21, 64
adjustable shelves, **35, 77**
air pockets, 28, *31*
antiquing, 40
antiquing furniture, **39**
arches, 60
artificial stones, 20
attic plan, *76*
attic room, **75, 90**
attics, 75
ATTICS AND BASEMENTS, 73

B

band saw, **89**
baseboard, **8**
basement stairway, **73**
basement walls, 7
basements, 73
bathroom paneling, 111
beams, 90, *91*
BEAUTY IN BOXES, 78
bedding compound, 41, 43
bi-fold doors, 32, **34**
blemishes, 19
box covering, **81**
brass hardware, **79**
breakfast nook, 65
brick, 20, 21
brick-in-a-can, 22
brick patterns, *20*
bricklaying, 20
bricklaying tools, *21*
brush or roller, 38
BUILD A COFFEE TABLE, 118, 119
butt joint, 79

C

cabinets, *36*
campaign chest hardware, **79**
carpet-covered box, **81**

caulking, **14**
cedar closet, **33**
cedar paneling, **63**
cedar shake wall, **64**
cedar shakes, **63**
ceilings, *17*
ceramic tiles, 54, 98
chalk line, **26**
chest, **83**
chimney, *46*
chopping block, **68**
clocks, 93, **94**
closet, *33*, 35
CLOSE-UP ON CEILINGS, 69
coffee table, 118, *119*
COMBINATION ROOM DIVIDER-FIREPLACE, 45
conditioning panels, 7
cork tiles, **20**
corners, *16*
cornice, 58
costs, 5
countertop, **67**
country living room, **92**
CREATE WITH SPINDLES, 113
cross tees, **72**
cube, **86**
curio cabinet, 89
curtains, 58
curved pictures, **97**
cutting panels, 9
cutting wallboard, **42**

D

dampness, 74
decals, 56
DECORATING WITH TAPE, 116
decorative hardware, **68**
desk, **103**
distressing, 40
dividers, **101, 102,** 103, **105**
do-it-yourself carpeting, 53
door removal, **30**
door sanding, **30**
doors and windows, **17**
dormer, 75
double-face tape, 28, 116
dry wall **40**
Dutch door, **68**

E

edge molding, 119
edging door, **31**
elbow room 36, **37**
electric fireplace, **46**
embossing, 116, 117
end table, **82**
expansion joints, 9

125

F

fabrics, 24
FABRICS FOR FASHIONABLE
  WALLCOVERINGS, 28
FACTORY-BUILT WALL-HUNG FIREPLACE, 44
factory finished moldings, 12
fake beams, 64, 70
fieldstone wall, 62
filigree panels, 60, 100, 102, *104*, **105**
fireplace divider, **45**
fireplace shimming, **47**
fireplace, wall-hung, **44**
flexible adhesive, **55**
floorcovering chart, 49, 51
flooring, 50
FOCUS ON FLOOR, 48
foil tape, 116, 117
foils, 25
framed moldings, **97**
fringe, 56
furring, 7, *10*, *11*, *12*

G

glaze, **40**
graining, **40**
grilles, removable, **107**
gypsum, 40

H

hand hewn beams, 64
hanger wires, **72**
heat seal, **57**
herringbone hardwood floor, **52**
horizontal panels, **15**
humidity, 106

I

inside corners, **16**
installing panels, 7
INSTALLING WALLBOARDS, 41, **42**
instant bricklaying, 20
INSTANT MAGIC, 121
instant stone, 62
island, kitchen, 65

J

joints, **43**

K

kitchen island, *65*
kitchen island ideas, *67*
KITCHEN CAPERS, 65
kitchen remodeling, 65
kitchen up-date, 66
knee wall, **76**

126

L

lambrequin, 59
laminated boxes, **78**
laminated window shades, **57**
laminating technique, *80*
latex-backed carpeting, **53**
latex type adhesive, 50
lazy susan, **66**
letters, 88
long nap roller, 40
loose plaster, **26**
louvered doors, **74**
low-relief tiles, 54
lumber dealer, **15**

M

maple top, 66
marking panels, 9
masonry walls, 7
mastic, 50, **52**
materials, **15**
MDO, 83
Mediterranean windows, 108
metal framework, **72**
mirrors, **87**
mitered frame, **96**
mitered joint, **84**
molding, cap, 12
molding, casing, 12
molding, cove, 12
moldings, prefinished, 9
moldings, removing, **8**
moldings, splicing, 12
moldings, various, *13*
moldings, working with, 11
mortar, **21**
mosaic tiles, **55**
mounting photos, 96
MOUNTING A PICTURE, 96
mural, **24**

N

nail heads, 41
nail popping, 41
nails, sheetrock, **43**
nautical room, **77**
NEW FOR THE BATHROOM, 109
notes on boxes, 82
novel uses for boxes, 82
no-wax floors, **48**

O

one-piece shower module, **109**
ornamental borders, *52*
outside corners, **9**, *14*
Oxford stone, 64

P

painting shades, 57
PAINTS AND PAINTING, 38
panel marking, 9
panel requirements, 7
panel starting, 9
panel, wood, **7**
paneling, bathroom, 111
panels, acclimating, **8**
panels, cutting, 9
pantry closet, 36
parquet, **83**
pecan panels, **7**
perforated tape, 43
photos, mounting, 96
pipes, 74
plank ceilings, 70
planning, 4
plastic-coated panel, **6**
plastic-finished panels, **19**
Plexiglas, **86**
plumb, **9**
plywood beams, **93**
ponderosa pine, 63
poured floors, 52
power saw, 9
power tools, **5**
pre-conditioning panels, **14**
pre-fabricated fireplace, 46
prefinished moldings, 9
pre-grooved moldings, 101
procedure, 9
protective backing, **31**
pull-out shelves, **35**

R

REMODELING, 4
removable grilles, **107**
roller or brush, 38
room dividers, 34, 100
RUSTIC DEN, 62, *64*

S

sanding wallboard, 42
screen divider, **100**
shade cloth, **57**
shading, 40
shag carpet, **99**
sheetrock nails, 42
shelf bracket, **89**
shelving, **34**, 35, **88, 99**
shims, **11**
shower cabinet, **110**
shutters, 58, 60
siding, **77**
sketches, 5
ski storage, **37**
SKIN FOR DULL DOOR, 30
slate top, 119
smoothing brush, **26**
spindles, 113, **114,** 115
splatter, 40
splintering, 9
spray adhesive, **61**
stenciling shades, 57
storage, 32
storage space, 65
STRETCH THAT STORAGE SPACE, 32
suspended ceiling, 71
switches, 25
swivel casters, **67**

T

tape, 22, 23, 116, 117
templates, **8**
textile paint, 57
textured panels, **6, 18**
tiles, ceramic, 85
tiles, resilient, 50
TIPS ON DIVIDERS, 100
tips on papering, 25
tongue and groove, **16**
tools for bricklaying, *21*
troweling, **22**

U

uneven walls, 11
untrue walls, 9

V

valance designs, *61*
valances, 58, *59*
varnish, 40
venting, 44, 47
vertical bands, 38
visualizing color, 38

W

WALL ACCESSORIES, 87
wallboard, 41
wallpaper applications, *27*, **99**
wallpapering materials, 24, *25*
WALLPAPERS AND FABRICS, 24
WALLS ARE FOR COVERING, 6
waterbase paints, 38
WHY WOOD WINDOWS, 106
WINDOW COVER-UPS, 56
window shade kit, **56**
window wall, 58
wood floors, 48
workshop, **5**
worm holes, 64

BUILD YOUR HOW-TO LIBRARY...

The experts tell you how-to-do-it-yourself in the all new hardcover Fawcett Practical Workshop Library, indexed for easy reference, filled with money-making ideas.

TV REPAIRS 051 • Save on service costs by doing it yourself! Shows the novice how to repair the 55 common things that can go wrong with a TV. Filled with step-by-step information on: picture tube replacement, how to get pure TV color, repairing TV sound, kill TV interference, fixing high voltage, UHF for older sets, cable TV, hidden components, horizontal and vertical problems, making antennas last.

PAINTING AND WALLPAPERING 056 • Complete guide to painting inside and out. This book covers when to use latex, acrylic or oil-base paint, how to buy and store rollers, preparing all interior surfaces, using spray paints and equipment, the new types of wall paper, where and how to caulk, special paints, preparing and painting exterior surfaces, handling gutters, downspouts, pipes, painting masonry and more.

CARPENTRY 052 • This book takes the novice from the basic workshop to the building of frame houses. Step-by-step illustrations and charts supplement the easy to understand text. Topics covered include: use of tools, safety, planning and constructing your home workshop, buying your lumber, paneling walls, tips on furniture building, adding new ceilings, installing built-ins, storage, adding rooms, and lots more.

FURNITURE REFINISHING, RESTYLING AND REPAIR 057 • Contains valuable information on know-how and correct procedures for professional looking restoration and repair of furniture. Topics include: Repairing dressers, tables, chairs, beautifying odd pieces, use of varnishes, making wood satin smooth, minor repairs, matching woods, restoring antiques and picture frames, stripping old finish, removing scratches, etc.

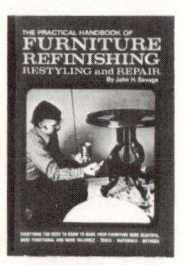

CONCRETE AND MASONRY 053 • Professional quality walks, drives, patios, walls, etc. can be made simply and inexpensively by using this handbook. It takes you through the rudiments of mixing and use of tools to the secrets of brick laying. Other topics include: the right way to use ready mix, mortar-making tips, beauty in stone, patching and resurfacing, casting footings, walls, floors, sidewalks and lots more.

CAR CARE AND REPAIR 058 • Top performance information, easy to follow and amply illustrated, that the average motorist will find extremely useful. Topics include: Paint and body work, basic tools every owner should have, buying parts, lubrication, tune-ups, electrical system, smooth shifting, valve grinds, overheating, exhaust system installation, overhaul tips, suspension, foreign cars, and much more.

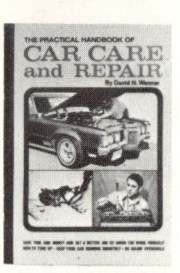

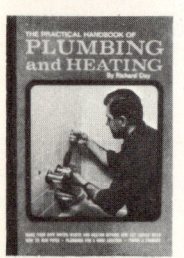

PLUMBING AND HEATING 054 • This book helps you cut those costly bills, by showing you how to do it yourself. It is filled with easy to understand drawings, charts and photos and contains a wealth of information. Topics include: saving heating dollars, disposal systems, learn your home plumbing system, waste and heating repairs, fixing a furnace, heating controls, necessary plumbing tools, and lots more.

REMODELING AND HOME IMPROVEMENTS 059 • Save money, add beauty and value to your home using this book. Aided by step-by-step illustrations and easy-to-follow how-to text, our expert author shows you how easy it is to: lower a ceiling, remodel a kitchen or bathroom, renovate a basement or attic, find and create storage space, install a fireplace, how to fix up or cover up windows, and more.

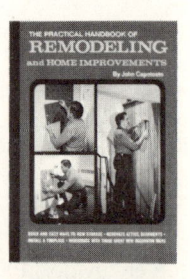

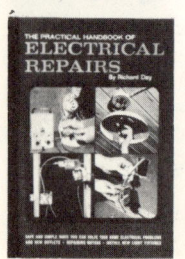

ELECTRICAL REPAIRS 055 • Filled with diagrams, pictures and easy-to-read charts, this is an indispensable guide to safe, simple ways to solve home electrical problems and to install new devices and wiring. Topics include: troubleshooting, repair of small and major appliances, safety, indoor/outdoor wiring and how to repair, installing light dimmers, fixing fluorescent lights, add new outlets and lots more.

STEREO AND HI-FI 060 • Written in an easy-to-follow style, this highly informative book will become a bible for every home, providing expert advice and know-how in selecting the best Stereo/Hi-Fi components, do-it-yourself kits. Topics include: Add Remote Speakers, Avoiding Transistor Damage, Convert to 4-Channel Stereo Without Electronics, Stereo Cabinets, Built-Ins, Dictionary of latest Stereo Definitions.

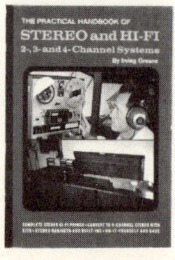

For further information on these and other Fawcett Books, please write: Fawcett Publications, Dept. PWL 059, Fawcett Place, Greenwich, Conn. 06830